"Christin Ditchfield really does have a way with words! Words are powerful to help, to heal, to encourage, and to inspire. I am inspired to make the most of my words as a result of Christin's wisdom and practical encouragements. Everyone would feel more ready for life and love by reading *A Way with Words*. I've pulled out my stationery and have my e-mails ready to send! I am writing those notes, sending those cards, and making those calls because I am well equipped by *A Way with Words*."

Pam Farrel, author, *Men Are like Waffles, Women Are like Spaghetti*; *Woman of Influence*; and *Woman of Confidence*

"Winsome, wise, witty. This is a book that every woman must read. Christin shows us that our words can either wound or heal, and she takes us on a soul-search to discover how to harness our words for redemptive purpose."

Jennifer Kennedy Dean, Executive Director, The Praying Life Foundation; author, *Live a Praying Life*

"*A Way with Words* is the most comprehensive study I've ever read on the importance of choosing to use the right words. Author Christin Ditchfield poignantly describes the power words have to hurt, heal, encourage, and inspire. If you long to communicate life, hope, and truth effectively, read this book."

Carol Kent, speaker; author, *When I Lay My Isaac Down*

"I love Christin Ditchfield's voice! On the platform. On the radio. In the pages of this book. Like the music of a gifted artist whose heart pours through the talented play of his or her instrument, Christin's heart pours skillfully through the words of this book, inviting us to use words well for God's glory and our joy. Digging deeply into the words of women of the Bible and the women of history, Christin renews our attention to one of the most important things about us—the way we use our power and freedom to speak to others. She calls us to something greater than freedom of speech: the honor of speech. How are we using words to show the love and majesty of God, to give a healing touch to others? How are we refraining from using words that are critical or useless? In today's world of word-overload, Christin challenges every woman to handle words like weapons, with great care, and like jewels, to adorn the lives of others."

Lael Arrington, author, *A Faith and Culture Devotional*, www.laelarrington.com

"*A Way with Words* will bring life to you. You can almost hear Christin's soothing voice flow through the pages, telling wonderful stories, quoting women as varied as Audrey Hepburn and Fanny Crosby, and backing it all solidly with Scripture."

Dee Brestin, author, *The Friendships of Women* and *The God of All Comfort*

"In my home I have a framed print that reads, 'Words are so powerful they should only be used to bless, to prosper, and to heal.' *A Way with Words* is a wonderful reminder of that truth. Thank you, Christin, for the challenge and blessing of *your* words."

Kendra Smiley, conference speaker; author, *Journey of a Strong-Willed Child*

"Christin, as always, reveals her heart, Scripture, and the importance of examining ourselves. *A Way with Words* is great for an individual or group study. The study questions at the end of each chapter cause you to reflect and examine Scripture and your heart. I recommend women of every age to read this book and 'Take It to Heart.'"

Tonya Appling, homeschool mom

"Though I've read other books and heard many sermons on the power of one's words, *A Way with Words* brought new conviction to my life in areas I hadn't considered in my daily dealings with my husband, children, and friends. This book should be required reading annually as a gentle reminder of our awesome responsibility as women regarding the power of our words. Though Christin and I have been friends for many years, I still stand in amazement at her God-given talent with words. I heartily thank her for not being afraid to speak the truth in love. *This* is a much needed truth."

Briggette, South Carolina, wife and mother of two

"Christin clearly illustrates the wonderful gift and great responsibility we have as women. I am both encouraged and challenged!"

Deborah Meacham, full-time caregiver

"This may be the most helpful women's book I have ever read—practical, accessible, and personal. Christin's words touched my heart and made me want to grow and bless every life that touches mine. I wish I had read this book years ago."

Daryl Ann Beeghley, fifty-three-year-old mother, grandmother, and veteran homeschool teacher

"*A Way with Words* is a must-read book to obtain victory in your life and set you free to fulfill your destiny. It will stir your thinking *before* you speak. When you think of the power of life or death in your tongue, this book will surely ignite the desire to use your words wisely and creatively in order to build up, create, encourage, influence, and love those around you."

Wendy

A Way with Words

What Women Should Know
about the Power They Possess

CHRISTIN DITCHFIELD

WHEATON, ILLINOIS

Library of Congress Cataloging-in-Publication Data
Ditchfield, Christin.
    A way with words : what women should know about the power they possess / Christin Ditchfield.
      p. cm.
    Includes bibliographical references.
    ISBN 978-1-4335-0284-2 (tpb)—ISBN 978-1-4335-2236-9 (ebk) 1. Oral communication—Religious aspects—Christianity. 2. Christian women—Conduct of life. I. Title.

BV4597.53.C64D58   2010
241'.672082—dc22

                                   2009039056

VP		21	20	19	18	17	16	15	14	13	12		11	10
14	13	12	11	10	9	8	7	6	5	4	3		2	1

For Briggette and Julie and Wendy and Deborah—
my kindred spirits, my sisters, my friends

Contents

One

Women Have a Way with Words

"Then the LORD God made a woman. . . ." (Gen. 2:22)

It was an experience I would never forget. Years ago, I was asked to take over the preschool program at a local Christian school, filling in for a teacher who was needed at a different grade level. On my first day I was introduced to the seven students in my class: six fun-loving, rambunctious little boys and one adorable little girl, Colby. After an hour of free playtime, I called all of the children over to the table to color a picture. Before I could set the big tub of crayons down in the center of the table, the six boys began diving for it—crawling up on the table to reach into it. I was caught off guard by their eagerness. In all the years I'd been teaching, I'd never seen such enthusiasm over a tub of crayons. The boys were practically coming to blows, scratching and clawing and slapping each other's hands away. For the life of me, I couldn't understand what all the fuss was about. There were hundreds of crayons in the bin—plenty for everyone. I understood even less when I realized they were fighting for the pink ones.

Every little boy in the class was determined to emerge from the bin with a pink crayon firmly in his grasp. It soon became clear that pink was Colby's favorite color. The boys wanted to color their own pictures pink, to imitate her, to earn her favor and approval. As the day went on, I learned that Colby ruled the class with a tiny velvet fist. All day long the boys competed to sit beside her, stand next to her—share the swings or the slide. She very sweetly dictated what games were played inside and out. Whenever I presented the boys with a choice of activity or course of action, they looked to Colby to see what she preferred. At four years old, Colby was the queen and every boy in the class her devoted servant. Her wish was their command.

"If the first woman God ever made was strong enough to turn the world upside down all alone, these women together ought to be able to turn it back, and get it right side up again!" —Sojourner Truth

It would take weeks of concerted effort on my part to loosen her grip—to gently dethrone Colby. (There could only be one "queen" in my classroom.) But it was an unforgettable experience, one that brought home to me a profound truth—the extraordinary power of a woman's influence. Barely out of babyhood, one little girl had the power to control and manipulate a classroom full of little boys. And she didn't have to be taught how. It's not as if she'd been to a seminar entitled "Learn to Get What You Want Today." She wasn't old enough to read, so she clearly hadn't gotten any tips from the self-help manuals on "winning friends and influencing people." She was born with the power to influence others. All women are. It's a God-thing.

> "The practice of putting women on pedestals began to die out when it was discovered that they could give orders better from there." —Betty Grable

"Then the Lord God made a woman . . ." (Gen. 2:22). The world has told women that for centuries they have been powerless—the hapless and helpless victims of a male-dominated society. Weak and inferior. But nothing could be further from the truth. It's true that down through history, in certain eras and cultures, formal education, professional careers, property ownership, and religious and political freedoms have been denied us. But we have never been powerless. From the very beginning—ever since Eve gave Adam that come-hither look in the garden of Eden—women have been having their way. And having their say. It's a truth so often reflected in centuries-old proverbs and colloquial expressions from around the world:

"Behind every great man is a woman."

"If Mama ain't happy, ain't nobody happy."

"The hand that rocks the cradle rules the world."

"The man may be the head of the house, but the woman is the neck—and she turns the head any way she wants."

Expressions like these acknowledge the reality that as women, we are in fact naturally gifted by God with great power and influence. We always have been. We always will. Sometimes we exert this power directly. Other times our influence is felt through the example that we set—or the way others are challenged or inspired or motivated as a result of their relationship to us.

In the 1800s, in a letter to his fiancée, Emilie, Army surgeon Walter Reed was moved to exclaim, "Oh the power of a woman's influence when the heart of man is brought into subjection through love! Her frown prostrates him in the dust; her smile lifts him to Heaven! Ah! Tell me of the brilliant accomplishments of man and I will tell you of a heart enchained! Tell me of an effort that knows no relaxation by day or night, and I will tell you of the power of a woman's influence. She can degrade him to the level of a brute; she can elevate him to the position of a god. How careful she should be in the use of this great influence!"[1] (Thanks in large part to Emilie's encouragement and support, Walter would one day become famous for making the groundbreaking discovery that mosquitoes transmit diseases like malaria and yellow fever—saving thousands, if not millions of lives as a result.)

"No one can make you feel inferior without your consent." —Eleanor Roosevelt

It's time we realized what an incredible privilege it is to be a woman . . . and what an awesome responsibility! As women, we have tremendous power—and not just over the men in our lives. Think about it: a woman's sphere of influence today is far more diverse and extensive than ever before. It doesn't start when (and if) we get married. It doesn't end when our children leave home. We are not only wives and mothers, but daughters, sisters, aunts, and grandmothers. We are coworkers, employers, and employees. Today we have unprecedented power in the entertainment industry, the corporate world, politics, and sports. Our influence has expanded in churches, our communities, our culture, and around the world!

And the way we wield that influence most often is with our words. Women have a way with words. It begins in toddlerhood, when linguistics experts note that nearly 100 percent of the sounds emanating from our mouths are conversational—in other words, "chit-chat." Not true for our little brothers and their friends. In fact, as much as 90 percent of their communication at the same age is unintelligible noise: "Vroom, vroom! Bang! Pow!"

> "I believe that it is as much a right and duty for women to do something with their lives as for men. . . ." —Louisa May Alcott

We women talk sooner, and we talk more. Way more. It's been suggested that the average adult man speaks as many as 25,000 words a day. The average woman: 50,000.[2] That's a staggering amount! What kind of words are we speaking? Words that build up, words that tear down. Words that guide and encourage and teach. Words that control and manipulate and deceive.

Remember the women who have spoken powerful words that have shaped your life. The words of a teacher who believed in you . . . a grandmother who faithfully prayed . . . a friend who took the time to listen—and then gave godly counsel—at a critical time in your life.

What about words that wounded you? Maybe your mother told you that you were a disappointment to her. Or you had a coach who ripped your performance to shreds. Remember the girls who teased you at school, who told you that you were too fat or too skinny or too tall. Or the boss who predicted you'd never make it in this business. Remember the things you've said to yourself in moments of discouragement or despair.

How have these words impacted you—for good or evil?

How have your words impacted others?

These are questions I've given a lot of thought to myself. I'm so grateful for the women who have encouraged me; I thank God for them. I have trouble forgiving and forgetting the words of those who have hurt me deeply. In fact, the only thing more painful to me than the memory of some of those words that have been spoken to me is the thought that I might have said the same kinds of things to others. A careless criticism or a thoughtless remark is all it takes to inflict that pain on someone else.

My parents (still!) proudly relate that I was a prodigious conversationalist with an extensive vocabulary by the time I was eighteen months old. According to my grandmother, I started preaching to my dollies when I was three. I wish that I could say all of my words have been biblical exhortation! But honestly, I've put my foot in my mouth more times than I care to remember. There are times when I said things I shouldn't—or didn't say things I should have.

> "Words—so innocent and powerless as they are, as standing in a dictionary, how potent for good and evil they become in the hands of one who knows how to combine them." —Nathaniel Hawthorne

It's something I struggle with daily, as does every woman I know. As many words as we speak in a day, it's no wonder. Proverbs 10:19 says, "When words are many, sin is not absent. . . ."

The Bible has a lot more to say about the power of our words and the battle to wield them wisely. The book of James observes,

> When we put bits into the mouths of horses to make them obey us, we can turn the whole animal. Or take ships as an example. Although they are so large and are driven by strong winds, they

are steered by a very small rudder wherever the pilot wants to go. Likewise the tongue is a small part of the body, but it makes great boasts. Consider what a great forest is set on fire by a small spark. The tongue also is a fire, a world of evil among the parts of the body. It corrupts the whole person, sets the whole course of his life on fire, and is itself set on fire by hell. All kinds of animals, birds, reptiles and creatures of the sea are being tamed and have been tamed by man, but no man can tame the tongue. It is a restless evil, full of deadly poison. With the tongue we praise our Lord and Father, and with it we curse men, who have been made in God's likeness. Out of the same mouth come praise and cursing. (James 3:3–10)

It's a sobering thought, one that begs the question: How are we doing in our efforts to "tame our tongues"? Are the words we speak words that wound or words that heal? Words that live or words that die? And what do our words reveal about our hearts?

It's really not overstating it to say that God has given us the incredible potential, the awesome privilege, and the amazing opportunity to impact the lives of those we love in a powerful way. It's up to us to make the most of it—to learn to use our words wisely and well.

Bible Study

At the end of each chapter, you'll find questions like these to help you reflect on the biblical principles presented and apply them to your own life. You'll want to record your responses in a separate notebook or journal.

1. Jot down the names of the women who—for better or worse—have had the most significant impact on your life. They may be women you have known intimately and personally for a long time or women who came in and out of your life very briefly. You may also include

women who have motivated you or inspired you from afar. Think about each one: how has her influence helped shape the woman you have become today?

2. Now list the names of the people whose lives you touch on a regular basis—friends and family members, coworkers, neighbors, etc. Think about some of the ways you influence them—the ways you interact with them and the kind of example you set.

3. Reread James 3:2–10. Which of the following statements best describes how you feel about "the power of the tongue" in your own life?

   ☐ I've never really thought much about it.

   ☐ I'm very aware of it. In fact, I'm actually kind of terrified of saying the wrong thing!

   ☐ This is an area of my life that I work really hard on. I know it's important.

   ☐ There are some aspects I've got under control; others I really struggle with.

   ☐ I realize that this is a major issue in my life. I need to do something about it.

4. Read Psalm 19:1–14. You may want to underline words or phrases that are meaningful to you. Then in your own words, summarize what each verse says.

   a. Of what does all creation "speak" (1–6)?

   b. Where do we find wisdom and instruction—not to mention joy and delight? Of what benefit is it to us (7–11)?

    c.   What two kinds of sin does the psalmist ask God to forgive and keep him from (12–13)?

5. This week, ask God to make you more aware of the power and influence he has given you, the opportunities you have to impact the lives of others. Pay attention to the kinds of words that come out of your mouth on a regular basis. Are they positive, uplifting, and beneficial to those who hear them? Or are they negative, unhelpful, even destructive?

6. If you haven't already, you may want to memorize the words of Psalm 19:14 and make it your special prayer this week:

> "May the words of my mouth and the meditation of
>   my heart
>   be pleasing in your sight,
>   O Lord, my Rock and my Redeemer."

7. Take a few moments to record any further thoughts in your notebook or journal.

Two

Words That Wound

"The wise woman builds her house, but with her own hands the foolish one tears hers down." (Prov. 14:1)

I could hear the weeping as I walked through the front door. I was in high school, and my mother had dropped me off for a weekend with my grandparents. I'd arrived a little early, and apparently my grandmother's Bible study group was still going strong. I tried to slip quietly past the living room and down the hall to the guest bedroom without disturbing them. As I did, I caught a glimpse of my grandmother standing in the center of the room, her body shaking with heart-rending sobs, her friends gathered around her, wrapping their arms around her and praying up a storm. Back in the bedroom, I unpacked my bag and glanced through a few books . . . and waited. When everyone had gone, my grandmother called me to come to the kitchen for a cup of tea. She didn't want me to be worried about what I had seen or heard. She explained that the Bible study had been about letting go of the hurts of the past, and that God had put his finger on a wound in her heart that needed to be healed—a burden from which she needed to be set free.

> "Woman is the salvation or the destruction of the family. She carries its destiny in the folds of her mantle." —Henri-Frederic Amiel

Still teary, my grandmother went on to tell me how she had realized that morning that there was a hurt she'd been holding onto ever since she was a little girl, something that had haunted her and hampered her all of her life. It seems that once, in a fit of anger, her mother had told her that she was a mistake and should never have been born. (Probably in reference to the fact that she'd been the reason her parents "had" to get married.) Her mother—my great-grandmother—was not a very sentimental woman; she had that stiff upper lip that the British are famous for. And this was long before she knew Jesus. I doubt if it would ever have occurred to her the anguish that her careless words could cause. But more than sixty years later, the pain was still so fresh that her daughter could hardly breathe. For decades her mother's words had hounded her. They robbed her of any sense of joy or satisfaction or fulfillment in her accomplishments. She'd become a national champion swimmer in her teens, an ambulance driver during World War II, and then a much-beloved wife and mother and grandmother. She was very active in the ministry of her church—always reaching out to younger women to welcome them and befriend them and mentor them. I can't count the number of these women who've told me how she touched their lives, how she blessed them and encouraged them. Yet in moments of weakness, at times when my grandmother was vulnerable, the devil used her mother's words to taunt her, to torment her, and to convince her that she was utterly useless and worthless, unwanted and unloved.

Wounded by words.

The world is full of women who have had their hopes shattered, their dreams dashed, their self-image left in shambles. Women who've been crippled or stifled or silenced by something hurtful that someone said to them. For some women, the wounds are more of a hindrance, an aggravation, a temporary setback, or a painful experience they eventually learn to "get over." Such an experience may even become a sort of catalyst that motivates and empowers a woman to rise to the challenge and prove her doubters and detractors wrong. But for every one of these, there are hundreds, if not thousands, who just can't get past the pain. Women who've been unable to enter into healthy relationships, unable to both give and receive unconditional love, because they've been convinced they aren't worthy of it. Women who've failed to live up to their potential or pursue their passion, who've refused to share their gifts and talents with others because someone once critiqued them harshly or accused them of being prideful or attention-seeking. Women who've literally starved themselves to death, because someone once told them they were fat. Women who have committed suicide to silence the critical voices that echoed endlessly in their heads.

As I've had the privilege of ministering to women across the country, I've heard so many of these stories—often told through tears. I have a few of my own. You probably do, too. Many of us know from firsthand experience that "sticks and stones may break our bones," but words can scar us for life.

Why is it then that we're not more careful with the words we speak to others? Why on earth would we choose to inflict that kind of pain on someone else?

I guess sometimes we just don't think. We don't realize what we're saying. We're careless, underestimating the power of our words and the impact they can have on others. Perhaps it doesn't occur to us to consider that someone else might have a different temperament or personality—a different sensitivity—

than we do, and might respond to what we're saying very differently than we would.

> "'Careful with fire' is good advice we know. 'Careful with words' is ten times doubly so." —William Carleton

It could be we don't think anyone is listening. We were just blowing off steam! Who pays attention to us anyway?

Maybe we're just trying to be cute or clever. Can't they take a joke?

The ugly truth is that sometimes our harsh words are deliberate. It's not an accident when we go on the attack. Our pride has been wounded, our plans have been frustrated, our anger is out of control. In those moments, we can't feel any pain but our own. All we know is that we've been hurt—and we want to hurt back. *Somebody* is going to pay! And it may be an innocent bystander.

On other occasions, we may actually think we're helping. We're very free with our opinions and advice, because we have what we feel are the best of intentions and we don't see anything wrong with putting in our two cents. We may even think we're doing God's will—like Rebekah.

It started with the birth of her twins, Esau and Jacob. In the midst of a difficult pregnancy, the babies constantly jostling each other, Rebekah received a prophecy, a word from the Lord: "Two nations are in your womb, and two peoples from within you will be separated; one people will be stronger than the other, and the older will serve the younger" (Gen. 25:23). In light of this prophecy and sensing God's hand on Jacob's life, Rebekah favored her youngest son. Scripture tells us plainly that she loved him more than she loved Esau. She protected Jacob and looked out for his interests. And if Jacob was called "the Deceiver," well, he learned a thing or two from his mother.

It was, after all, Rebekah who came up with the elaborate plan to help Jacob deceive his father and brother and steal Esau's birthright. "Now, my son, listen carefully and do what I tell you" (Gen. 27:8). It was bad advice that Rebekah gave her beloved son. Very bad. It showed contempt for her husband and a total lack of motherly love and compassion for her first-born. Perhaps there was some hurt and bitterness in her heart after years of family squabbles. But more than likely, her intentions were good. She thought she was doing the right thing. She was just trying to help God along—and fulfill in the flesh the prophecy she received during her pregnancy. After all, God had said that her older son would one day "serve the younger." Rebekah was so confident in her course of action that when Jacob expressed qualms about the possibility of being *cursed* instead of blessed by the scheme, Rebekah actually said: "My son, let the curse fall on me. Just do what I say. . . ."

Reckless words.

Rebekah's well-intended but poorly-considered advice proved disastrous—because God doesn't need any help. He never rewards scheming and manipulation. The curse did fall on Rebekah. Her deception was exposed. She irreparably damaged her relationship with her husband. And she lost both of her precious sons that day. Her older son bitterly resented her for her interference; her younger son had to flee across the country to escape his brother's wrath. Rebekah would never see him again, as long as she lived. Proverbs 14:1 observes: "The wise woman builds her house, but with her own hands the foolish one tears hers down."

Zeresh is an even better (or worse) example. Remember the story of Zeresh? We usually refer to it as the story of Esther— but Scripture points out that Zeresh played an important role. And not a good one. Her husband Haman was a man consumed with pride. He sought to destroy the entire Jewish race for what he perceived to be an insult from one man, Mordecai, who was Esther's cousin. If you read through the story in Esther 5–6, you might notice something. Haman did not come up with any of his evil schemes on his own. Three times we're told very specifically that Haman confided in his wife, Zeresh (along with their friends), and that they advised him what to do (Est. 5:10, 14; 6:13). As Haman complained about his wounded pride and railed against his Jewish enemies, his wife made no attempt to calm him down or try to help him keep things in perspective. She had no words of loving reassurance to soothe his ego. She didn't express her own admiration or respect for him. Instead, she egged him on and encouraged him to give full vent to his anger. Zeresh goaded her husband to seek revenge. But when the plan started to fall apart, she turned on him and made the dire pronouncement that it was hopeless; all was lost: "You will surely come to ruin!" (Est. 6:13). Talk about kicking a man when he's down!

I can't help but wonder if his wife's words weren't ringing in his ears, piling on the desperation that caused Haman to grab hold of the queen to plead for his life, a foolish move that, when it was misinterpreted, cost him his life. It was Zeresh who had come up with the idea to build the seventy-five-foot gallows on which Haman intended to have Mordecai hanged—the gallows on which Haman himself would be hanged, along with all ten of his sons. Her sons (Est. 7:10; 9:13).

"The tongue has the power of life and death, and those who love it will eat its fruit" (Prov. 18:21). We tend to think of "words that wound" consisting primarily of nasty name-calling and cruel insults. But as Rebekah and Zeresh show us, there are other ways our words become weapons. Let's take a look at a few of the most popular in our arsenal:

Unsolicited (and Often Unbiblical) Advice. We've just seen two powerful examples of this. I'll just add here that I don't think I've ever been to a grocery store or a salon or a party or a Bible study where I didn't hear at least one woman say to another:

"You know what you should do. . . ." I'm sure I've been guilty more than a few times myself. But if the other person hasn't asked for our help, even the most well-meaning counsel can come across as insensitive or intrusive. It may feel like a rebuke. Or add confusion and tension and stress to someone who is already overwhelmed and unsure of which path to take. We may not have all the facts needed to make truly wise and thoughtful suggestions. We haven't necessarily taken time to seek God for his direction for this particular person or circumstance. All too often, caught up in the moment, we find our "sage advice" is really nothing more than a flip response, an emotional reaction, or words of wisdom from Oprah, Dr. Phil, or the women's magazines at the checkout counter, rather than the Word of God itself. The consequences can be devastating.

Not-So-Constructive Criticism. For many of us this is a tough one, because we really mean for our criticism to be constructive. We want our little comments and suggestions to motivate our loved ones and inspire them to change (for the better, of course). But too often, they only devalue and demoralize and deflate. We could devote the rest of this book to a discussion of all the less-than-helpful things that well-meaning mothers have said to their daughters regarding their appearance, their career choice, their boyfriend or husband or lack thereof, their children or lack thereof. Instead of encouraging them, we push them and pressure them. We say we just want our loved ones to be happy. But how can they be, when what they hear from us is that they are unacceptable and unlovable the way they are now? They get the message that they're a disappointment to us; they've let us down.

It's been said that some people find fault like there was a reward for it. I think it's true. If we're not careful, we can get in the habit of constantly criticizing other people, finding fault with them and tearing them down, for no good reason. You know, there is actually a reward—a "finder's fee"—for this kind of critical attitude and approach to others. We do get something from it. When all we see is the "bad" in people, we get a heavy spirit. We get a reputation for being a nasty, negative person. We get lots of time to ourselves, because nobody wants to be around us. And we get God's solemn promise that he will one day hold us to the same impossible standard to which we've held others (Matt. 7:1–5).

Truth Not Spoken in Love. Just because something is true doesn't mean it's always kind or loving or helpful or even appropriate to say it. This includes bludgeoning others with Scripture in a misguided attempt to set them straight. Much of what Job's friends said was technically true—only it didn't apply to his specific circumstances, and it was hardly comforting, encouraging, or uplifting. A woman I know once felt like Job. Very suddenly her family found itself facing one crisis after another: loss of a job, death of an elderly parent, adult daughter attempting suicide, and adult son going through a divorce. To top it all off, she and her husband both came down with bronchitis. When, for the first time in five weeks, they were finally able to attend church, they slipped into the pew exhausted and desperate for some spiritual nourishment. Within minutes they were accosted by a woman, barely more than an acquaintance, determined to take them to task for their recent absence. "I've noticed you haven't been coming to church lately," she began. "The Bible says we're not supposed to 'give up meeting together.' We're all busy, but we have to make it a priority. You need to make a commitment to be here." She added, "I'm just telling you this because we're supposed to 'speak the truth in love.'" Seriously? There was no love behind her words. She was just being a busy-body. Love would have said, "It's so good to see you. We've missed you. How have you been?" And later, "How can we help?"

"Humor" That Gets Out of Hand. We were just teasing. Being a smarty-pants. Having a little fun. Then it got out of hand. Sarcasm has a place, for sure; it serves a purpose. It can be an effective tool to highlight hypocrisy and humble the proud and

arrogant. (God uses a fair amount of it himself.) But it's not meant to be used to constantly ridicule and rip to shreds people we claim we love. Even when our quips are clearly intended to be funny, even when they're accompanied by laughter, a daily barrage of put-downs or cut-downs or snarky asides can be brutal to another person's self-esteem. Even those of us who regularly enjoy a little "witty repartee" have to admit how quickly "cute" and "clever" can become ugly and grow old. As Benedick complained when he'd had enough of this kind of exchange with Lady Beatrice in Shakespeare's *Much Ado about Nothing,* "She speaks poniards [daggers], and every word stabs."

> "The real art of conversation is not only to say the right thing at the right place but to leave unsaid the wrong thing at the tempting moment." —Dorothy Nevill

Add a little sarcasm to a compliment and you can steal all the pride and joy, the enthusiasm, and the sense of accomplishment right out of someone else's heart. "Wow! You cleaned your room for once. Too bad it doesn't look this good every day." Or, "Your teacher says you're so organized and disciplined at school—wish you could be that way at home!" A favorite excuse: "We're not laughing *at* you; we're laughing *with* you." Really?

Gossip. We'll explore gossip more in chapter 6 because of its relationship to and effect on our own hearts and minds. But I want to mention it here, because it is one of the ways we wound others, and not just when what we've said somehow gets back to them! When we openly discuss and freely pass judgment on others' private struggles and personal tragedies, we are shaping public opinion about them. We are exposing them to further judgment and criticism and ridicule, often with more far-reaching effects than we can imagine. More than once, to my shame and regret, I've come to realize that I've avoided or ignored or actively disliked a person who could have been (or once was) a friend, simply because of what someone else had said about them. Have my own careless comments had the same effect on others? "A perverse man stirs up dissension, and a gossip separates close friends" (Prov. 16:28).

Casting up the Past. According to the dictionary, to cast is to "throw or hurl or fling." That's what we do when we cast up the past. We get into an argument, and we throw in people's faces every mistake they've ever made, every sin they've ever committed. We remind them over and over of their greatest moral failure, their most humiliating defeat. It's our way of putting them in their place or pointing out why they can't expect us to trust them. God says he's forgiven and forgotten, but we haven't—and we want to be sure they know it. They might think they have good news, an exciting opportunity, or hope for the future. We think we're doing them a favor by bursting their bubble and reminding them of how wrong they've been before. Believe it or not, there is someone whose official job is to cast up the past, to throw it in everyone's face: his name is Satan. The Bible calls him "the accuser of our brothers," because that's what he does day and night (Rev. 12:10). He works overtime to torment believers with the memory of sins and failures that have long been covered by the blood of Jesus. Do we really want to be his helpers?

The Silent Treatment. Strangely enough, one of the ways we wound with our words is to withhold them! When we refuse to communicate our thoughts and feelings, when we won't say what it is we're upset about or what people have done wrong, we shut them out. We fill their hearts with anxiety and frustration and even dread. We make them feel isolated and alienated and rejected—without saying a single word. And that is after all, what the silent treatment is for. Not to be confused with taking time out or having a cooling off period, the silent treatment is all about manipulation and control. It's a form of punishment or revenge that somehow feels more righteous than an angry outburst. But throwing this kind of tantrum is not the mark of an emotionally healthy, spiritually mature woman. It certainly isn't biblical (see Matt. 18:15–17).

These are just a few of the weapons at our disposal; they go on and on.

If only we could just compile a list of words and phrases we should never say! Then we could easily avoid them, right? Unfortunately, it's not that simple. What makes a word harmful often depends on how it's said, to whom, and in what context. For instance, "You're just like your father!" can be a wonderful compliment or a cruel barb.

"Painful as it may be, a significant emotional event can be the catalyst for choosing a direction that serves us—and those around us—more effectively. Look for the learning." —Louisa May Alcott

It's not just what's in our heart, but what's in the heart of the person we're speaking to. We can't always know when we've touched on a sensitive area. We may have no idea we're pouring salt in an open wound. Some of us tend to be more blunt, more candid, even confrontational in our communication with others. We have to understand that just because a comment wouldn't hurt our feelings doesn't mean it wouldn't or shouldn't hurt somebody else's. If, everywhere you go, you leave behind you a trail of bloody wounded, don't expect to stand before Jesus and blame everyone else for being "too sensitive."

On the other hand, there are times when—no matter how kind and considerate and gentle we try to be—some people will take offense. I've known more than one woman who looked at life through "everybody-hates-me" glasses. You could say to her, "It's such a beautiful day!" And she would hear, "Too bad you're so ugly." It's sad. But it's her problem, not ours. At the end of the day, there really isn't anything we can do about it—other than pray for her and try to love her anyway.

There will be people who purposely twist our words, deliberately misunderstand us, and willfully take offense where none was intended. Many of these folks have been so warped by the wounds they have suffered that they are incapable of seeing and hearing clearly. Others are just plain evil. And that's a fact. Jesus warned us that we would be hated by some people simply because of our love for him (Mark 13:13; Luke 6:22). Our faith itself is offensive to them. It convicts them of their own sinfulness, and they don't like it (2 Cor. 2:14–16). It's the truth that offends them, not us.

So what *are* we responsible for? What *can* we do? As it turns out, plenty. But it doesn't have to be an overwhelming or impossible task. Here are a few steps to get you headed in the right direction:

1. Pay attention! If you haven't already, start now. Listen to the words that are coming out of your mouth. Are they kind and loving and helpful? Or are they harsh and critical and judgmental? Imagine you were the star of your own reality TV show. If those camera crews were following you around 24/7, what would they catch on tape? As you go about your day, ask God to make you much more aware of the words you speak and the power they have to impact the people you come in contact with.

2. Take responsibility for taming your own tongue. You're not responsible for what other people say. Or even how they respond to you. You are responsible before God to make an effort to tame *your* tongue. "If it is possible, as far as it depends on you, live at peace with everyone" (Rom. 12:18). Pray with the psalmist, "Set a guard over my mouth, O Lord; keep watch over the door of my lips" (Ps. 141:3). Memorize other verses that remind you of what God says about the power of the tongue and how we are to wield that power.

Identify situations in which you're most tempted to lose control and speak out of turn. Then come up with a strategy for how you'll handle those situations in the future. For instance, you might go for a walk or run errands during your lunch break instead of sitting around the lunchroom trading office gossip. Brainstorm ahead of time things you can say to change the subject of a conversation when a friend takes it in a direction you know you shouldn't go. If you tend to be overly critical of your family, make a list of the positive things that you appreciate about each one and then make a point of complimenting them on those things. Ask a trusted friend or family member to hold you accountable and help you with this. One of my friends has worked out signals with her husband that they use to help each other in social situations. When she starts dominating a conversation and giving unsolicited advice, he gently squeezes her shoulder. When he gets too loud and argumentative, she pats his knee. Together they keep each other on course.

Set some boundaries. Years ago, I made a decision not to tease people I don't like—because I realized I couldn't stop myself from skewering them with sarcasm. On the surface it sounded as though it was all in good fun, but there was real venom underneath, which meant there was a good chance someone would really get hurt. These days I only tease people I know and dearly love, because the affection I feel for them keeps me from being cruel or unkind. I know to avoid things they're truly sensitive about. I also know they're much more likely to call me on it by confronting and correcting me if I go too far. When I need to vent my frustrations, there are certain people I seek out and certain people I avoid. I know I need a listener who will be empathetic and understanding, but not encourage me to sin. And I need someone whose faith in or friendship with others won't be shaken by what I have to say.

The strategies and boundaries will be different for each one of us, just as the temptations are. But God has promised to give us all the wisdom and courage and strength we need to win this battle if we ask him for it (James 1:5; 1 Cor. 10:13; Heb. 4:15–16)!

3. Whenever possible—as soon as possible—ask forgiveness of those you have wounded with your words. Offer a sincere and heartfelt, "I'm sorry. I was wrong. Please forgive me." Say it in person, over the phone, or in writing—whatever is most appropriate, given the circumstances. Humble yourself and admit to the other person (your husband, the kids, your neighbor, a coworker, or friend) that this is an area where you realize you really struggle—it's something you're working on. Tell them the steps you're taking to get control over your tongue. Ask them to be patient with you and work with you to help you to stay on track.

"An apology is the superglue of life. It can repair just about anything." —Lynn Johnston

Of course, there are some words we can't take back. Some mistakes we can't undo. It may not be possible to contact every person we've ever wounded; it may not even be appropriate in every situation! But we can certainly ask God for *his* forgiveness. If the other person is still living, we can ask him to bless them wherever they are and heal them of any hurt we have caused. We can make a point of learning from our mistakes, so that we don't make the same ones over and over again in our relationships with others.

4. Forgive those whose words have wounded you. They may have no idea of the pain they have caused you; then again, they might. But whether they ever apologize or not, you've got to forgive them. You've got to let go of the pain, the bitterness, and resentment. Scripture tells us, "Therefore, as God's chosen people, holy and dearly loved, clothe yourselves with compassion, kindness, humility, gentleness and patience. Bear with each other and forgive whatever grievances you may have against one another. Forgive as the Lord forgave you" (Col. 3:12–13).

The truth is that at some point or another, we've all spoken thoughtlessly, reacted in anger or frustration, blurted out things we don't mean, said things we regret or repent of later. We need God and others to forgive us. Therefore, we need to extend God's forgiveness to others (Matt. 6:14–15; 18:21–35). Please understand: I'm not saying it's easy. It isn't. But whenever I'm tempted to tell God it's too hard—the offense is too great, the wound is too deep—I remember the story of Corrie ten Boom.

Corrie and her sister Betsie were arrested for hiding Jews in their home during the Nazi occupation of Holland. They were sent to a concentration camp, where they experienced unspeakable suffering and torment. Corrie was later released, and for years afterward she traveled the world, testifying to God's sustaining grace. One day after speaking at a church service, Corrie came face to face with one of her former prison guards. The man had become a Christian, and he wanted to ask her to forgive him for his cruelty at the prison camp. At that moment, all of the awful memories came rushing back in vivid detail.

"My blood seemed to freeze," Corrie said later. "And I stood there—and could not. Betsie had died in that place—could he erase her slow terrible death simply for the asking?"

The seconds seemed like hours, as Corrie wrestled with the most difficult thing she ever had to do. "For I had to do it," she said. "I knew that. The message that God forgives has a prior condition: that we forgive those who have injured us. 'If you do not forgive men their trespasses,' Jesus says, 'neither will your Father in Heaven forgive your trespasses.'"

"Still I stood there with the coldness clutching my heart. But forgiveness is an act of the will, and the will can function regardless of the temperature of the heart. 'Jesus, help me!' I prayed silently. 'I can lift my hand. I can do that much. You supply the feeling.'"

Suddenly, the healing power of God flooded Corrie's entire being. With tears in her eyes, she cried out, "I forgive you, brother. . . . With all my heart!" Corrie said, "I had never known God's love so intensely as I did then."[1]

What an incredible testimony! I honestly believe that if Corrie could forgive, then so can we—for that same healing power, the power of God, is available to us today.* For our own sakes, as much as for others, we must choose to forgive.

Over the years, God has made me so keenly aware of my own shortcomings in this area. I've shed many tears over words I wish I'd left unsaid. I'm so very thankful for the blood of Jesus that cleanses us from all our sin, all our "unrighteousness" (1 John 1:9). And that God's grace is sufficient for us (2 Cor. 12:9). His mercies are new every morning (Lam. 3:23). Each day offers us a fresh start.

For myself, I'm determined to learn and grow through all of this and let it make me a better woman, not a bitter one. I'm going to lay aside those words that wound—in favor of words that heal.

Bible Study

1. Think about the conversations you participate in on a daily basis—at home, at work, and at church. Things you say to yourself, things you say to family and friends. Words you speak in person or on the

---

*If your wounds are very deep—if, for instance, you've been the victim of verbal abuse or you've been struggling many years to get past your past—let me encourage you to contact your pastor or women's ministry leader or a Christian counselor, someone who can walk alongside you and help you on your journey to healing. You might also find help through some of the recommended resources listed in the back of this book.

phone. Things you write in e-mails or post on message boards and blogs. Which of these "weapons" do you find you most often wield?

☐ Unsolicited (and often unbiblical) advice

☐ Not-so-constructive criticism

☐ Truth not spoken in love

☐ "Humor" that gets out of hand

☐ Gossip

☐ Casting up the past

☐ The silent treatment

2. Read Ephesians 4. You may want to underline words or phrases that are meaningful to you. Then answer the questions below.

   a. What kind of words should describe us as followers of Christ (2, 13, 23–24, 32)?

   b. What kind of words *should not* come out of our mouths (25, 29, 31; see also Eph. 5:4)?

   c. What kind of words *should* come out of our mouths (15, 25, 29, 32; see also Eph. 5:4)?

3. Ask the Holy Spirit to show you if there is someone you have wounded with your words, someone whose forgiveness you need to seek. You may know right away, or you may find that God brings someone to mind later on. Whenever it happens, determine that you will act on what God has revealed. Pray for wisdom about whether to call or write or speak in person. Consider whether you owe the person a public or private

apology. (Generally if a sin is committed in private, the apology should be private; if it is committed in public, the apology should be public.) As painful as the thought of humbling ourselves and confessing our sin may be, it's not nearly as painful as carrying around the weight of guilt and shame. No matter how our apology is received, we can be at peace, knowing that our conscience is now clear. We have done what we could to make things right. We have been obedient to God's Word. We have his forgiveness, his mercy and grace.

4. Read Matthew 6:14–15. Is there someone you need to forgive? Whether they know they have wronged you or not, whether the wound was intentional or not, whether they ever apologize or not, make a commitment (and reaffirm it as often as necessary) that you will let go of the hurt and pain, and choose to forgive. Write a statement expressing this commitment.

5. Prayerfully consider that in some circumstances, Scripture says we have a responsibility to go to other people and let them know that they have hurt us, so that they have the opportunity to apologize, and there can be healing and reconciliation in the relationship (see Matt. 18:15–17). Be sure that your heart is in the right place, that your goal is not simply to get things off your chest or to get even, but to offer forgiveness and restoration.

6. Choose one of the following verses (or one mentioned previously in the chapter) to memorize and meditate on this week. Copy it on a note card or sticky note and attach it someplace where you will see it often—on the bathroom mirror, the refrigerator, the car dashboard,

alongside your computer screen or television, or next to the phone.

Psalm 15:1–3	Proverbs 18:21
Psalm 141:3	Ephesians 4:29
Proverbs 10:19	Philippians 2:14–15
Proverbs 13:3	2 Timothy 2:23–25
Proverbs 15:1	1 Peter 2:21–23
Proverbs 15:28	2 Peter 3:15–16

7. Take a few moments to record any further thoughts or reflections.

Three

Words That Heal

"Reckless words pierce like a sword, but the tongue of the wise brings healing." (Prov. 12:18)

Over and over it happens. I find myself sitting in a fancy ballroom or a church fellowship hall elaborately decorated with swaths of shimmering fabric, beautiful flower arrangements, twinkly lights, and tall candles. Sometimes there's a trellis or a waterfall, a hand-painted mural, or dozens and dozens of potted plants. A hush has fallen over the room, but underneath it there's a buzz of excitement and anticipation. A few feet away, a woman is standing at the podium, saying all kinds of wonderful things about me—who I am and what I've accomplished and why she's invited me here to speak. As she continues, I glance over at the sea of faces before me: beautiful faces. The faces of precious women who are desperate to hear a word from the Lord. On the outside, they all look perfectly put-together. But I know that, statistically speaking, many of them must be really struggling. Some of them will have just lost a loved one—a parent, a child, a spouse. Others will have cancer or some other life-threatening disease. *Maybe they just found out this week.* Some of them will be going through a divorce or trying to recover from one. Some have prodigal children. Others are under tremendous financial stress. They may have lost their jobs or their home. *They're hanging on by a thread.* Some have been coming to church for years and still don't really understand what the excitement is about—why everyone else seems so enthused about attending Sunday school or small group Bible studies, going on and on about "Jesus this" and "Jesus that." Others were invited by a friend or coworker and have never been to a church-sponsored event before. *They have no idea what to expect.*

> "If I can stop one heart from breaking, I
> shall not live in vain." —Emily Dickinson

In my mind I start going over the message I've prepared, asking God to guide me and give me the right words to say, hoping and praying it will be just what these women need. I'm overwhelmed both by the privilege and the responsibility of it all. For a moment the room fades, and suddenly I'm twelve years old again. Wildly curly, unmanageable red hair, freckles all over my face, great big glasses. Awkward and uncoordinated. Lonely and shy. Paralyzed by fears far too numerous to list here. And yet there's a longing in my heart for something I can't even put into words. It's a desire to serve God somehow and proclaim his truth . . . though I don't have the courage to speak to the kids at school or ask a saleswoman or a librarian for help. I hear my grandmother calling me over to the breakfast table, where she's just been reading her Bible and talking to Jesus. "Christin," she says, putting her arm around me and pulling me close, "I just know that God has a special call on your life. Whenever I pray for you, I get these visions in my mind's eye. I see you speaking to thousands and thousands of people."

Sitting on the platform, I remember how wonderfully mysterious—yet ridiculously impossible—it seemed back then. But here I am today. *With God, nothing is impossible.* My eyes fill with tears and a sob catches in my throat. I'm bursting with awe and joy and gratitude. The emotion threatens to knock me over like a tidal wave. But I can't give in to it; the applause has begun, and it's time for me to make my way to the lectern. As I open my Bible, I pause for a half second to offer a silent, wordless prayer of thanksgiving. Then, with a deep breath, I begin to speak. . . .

My grandmother is with Jesus now; I'm so thankful she got to see the beginning of my ministry, the firstfruits in answer to her faithful prayers. (I can't wait to tell her the rest!) I can't even begin to list all the others down through the years who have prayed for me and believed in me and spoken words of encouragement to my heart. My parents, my aunts and uncles, my youth pastor and his wife, the missionary who visited our church that one Sunday. The teachers who challenged me, the authors who inspired me, the friends who comforted me. They gave me godly counsel and advice and they corrected me when I got out of line. Many continue to do so to this day! I'm in awe of how God has used these people (very often and especially other women) to help me grow in my relationship with him, to prepare me and equip me to answer his call. They have a part in every life I touch—and every life that is touched by the women God has touched through me. The echoes are endless.

A woman's words can do so much more than wound. They can motivate and encourage and inspire. They can comfort, strengthen, and heal. They can promote repentance and forgiveness, restoration and reconciliation. They even have the power to avert disaster, to prevent travesties and tragedies from taking place.

In all of Scripture, I don't think you can find a better example of this power for good—the power of a wise woman's words—than in the story of Abigail in 1 Samuel 25. At the time, King Saul had already been warned that his disobedience had cost him his kingdom. The prophet Samuel anointed David to replace him. But Saul was not about to go away quietly. Instead he decided to hunt David down and kill him, determined to thwart God's plan and prevent the shepherd-boy turned giant-slayer from taking his throne.

For years, David lived on the run, hiding from the armies of Saul in the mountains and the deserts of Israel and its surrounding countries. He was not alone; he had an army of his own. Over six hundred fighting men—mighty warriors—had rallied to him, eagerly anticipating the day God would give him the kingdom. Until such time, David had to find ways to support them and him. In the Desert of Maon, David and his men offered protection to local farmers, guarding their servants and their flocks from Philistine marauders—a valuable service, free of charge. Then at harvest time, David made what was clearly an appropriate and reasonable request. He asked one of the farmers, Nabal, to share some of his prosperity, to give David and his men a meal as thanks for all of their hard work. Unfortunately, in this instance, he was most rudely rebuffed. The ingrate snubbed David and publicly ridiculed and insulted him. Enraged, the man who would be king gathered his army and prepared to launch a full-scale attack on the ignorant, belligerent peasant farmer.

But the farmer had a wife, Abigail, whom Scripture describes as "an intelligent and beautiful woman." She heard what had happened and immediately rode out to meet David and his men, bringing with her enough food to feed an army (literally!). Yet the greatest gift to David was the godly counsel that came out of her mouth. Scripture says,

> When Abigail saw David, she quickly got off her donkey and bowed down before David with her face to the ground. She fell

at his feet and said: "My lord, let the blame be on me alone. Please let your servant speak to you; hear what your servant has to say. May my lord pay no attention to that wicked man Nabal. He is just like his name—his name is Fool, and folly goes with him. [In this case, this was simply a statement of fact, an acknowledgment of guilt—not a gratuitous insult.] But as for me, your servant, I did not see the men my master sent.

"Now since the Lᴏʀᴅ has kept you, my master, from bloodshed and from avenging yourself with your own hands, as surely as the Lᴏʀᴅ lives and as you live, may your enemies and all who intend to harm my master be like Nabal. And let this gift, which your servant has brought to my master, be given to the men who follow you. Please forgive your servant's offense, for the Lᴏʀᴅ will certainly make a lasting dynasty for my master, because he fights the Lᴏʀᴅ's battles. Let no wrongdoing be found in you as long as you live. Even though someone is pursuing you to take your life, the life of my master will be bound securely in the bundle of the living by the Lᴏʀᴅ your God. But the lives of your enemies he will hurl away as from the pocket of a sling. When the Lᴏʀᴅ has done for my master every good thing he promised concerning him and has appointed him leader over Israel, my master will not have on his conscience the staggering burden of needless bloodshed or of having avenged himself. . . ." (1 Sam. 25:23–31)

Abigail began her appeal with the most humble of apologies, acknowledging the call of God on David's life and his right to be angry over her husband's foolishness. Then she reminded David that the Lord would fight his battles and deal with his enemies. She gently suggested that he reflect on the potential consequence of the sin he was about to commit. Abigail urged David to ignore her husband—forgive and forget Nabal's foolishness—and focus instead on his own destiny as Israel's next king.

Listen to the response: "David said to Abigail, 'Praise be to the Lᴏʀᴅ, the God of Israel, who has sent you today to meet me. May you be blessed for your good judgment and for keeping me from bloodshed this day and from avenging myself with my own hands. Otherwise, as surely as the Lᴏʀᴅ, the God of Israel, lives, who has kept me from harming you, if you had not come quickly to meet me, not one male belonging to Nabal would have been left alive by daybreak'" (1 Sam. 25:32–35).

To think what might have happened if Abigail had not had the courage to speak up! Or worse, what if she had heaped fuel on the fire by arguing with David, criticizing him and condemning him, or even encouraging him to destroy her foolish husband? Thankfully she took a different path; she chose a much better approach. And David took Abigail's words to heart. He recognized the wisdom of her counsel and thanked God for sending her to him. Abigail not only saved her own life and the lives of her family, but David's as well. Later, when her husband died, David married her. He wasn't about to let a woman like that get away!

> "Kind words can be short and easy
> to speak, but their echoes are truly
> endless." —Mother Teresa

Proverbs 12:18 says, "Reckless words pierce like a sword, but the tongue of the wise brings healing." Scripture is full of examples and illustrations of this truth—how the right words spoken at the right time (and often by women) have the power to touch hearts and lives and change the course of history. In a good way.

In a sense these words, too, are like weapons. But they don't skewer *people*. They're used to combat evil, to cut through fear and doubt, delusion, discouragement, and despair. We use these weapons to fight off the enemy and counteract the damage he would do to those we love. Here are some of the best weapons we have at our disposal:

Godly Counsel and Biblically-Grounded Advice. In a time of crisis, in a moment of need, when someone comes to us with a problem, when we can see that someone is headed for danger or disaster, it's often our opportunity and our privilege to speak into their lives, to pierce through the darkness and confusion, and to point them to the Light. Sometimes it's a special, one-time occurrence—a "divine appointment" of sorts; with others, we'll have the opportunity over and over again. (We'll talk more about teaching and training and mentoring in chap. 10). Often we can draw on our own life experiences—our failures, as well as our successes. There are things we have learned from wise people we've encountered and things we've learned all on our own (often the hard way). But most important are the things God has taught us in the pages of his Word, the biblical principles that are the foundation of our life and faith. It's so critically important that the wisdom we impart is not merely human wisdom or earthly wisdom, but "the wisdom that comes from above." The Bible tells us it's easy to recognize this kind of wisdom, because it is pure, peace-loving, gentle at all times, willing to yield to others, full of mercy and good fruit, impartial, and sincere (James 3:17). This wisdom may be called for suddenly and unexpectedly or quite naturally and frequently over the course of the day. We can be prepared by making sure we spend time daily in God's presence, studying his Word, seeking his face, asking him to give us his wisdom—to fill us with it—so that whenever we need it, it's there.

Truth Spoken in Love. Often it's said rather flippantly, "The truth hurts!" And sometimes it does. It can be painful, especially when it exposes an area of weakness or self-delusion or sin. But it's a lot easier to swallow if it's spoken in love. The fact is, some situations call for us to correct others and hold them accountable for their actions or behavior. Other circumstances require us to uphold a standard (especially a biblical standard) and call others to repentance and a return to obedience to God's Word. Most often, this takes place in conversation or confrontation with people with whom we have a deeply personal relationship—those we know intimately, with whom we have established trust and earned the right to speak. In any case, this kind of loving correction should only be undertaken prayerfully and with great care and concern. It shouldn't give us any joy. If we feel even a hint of triumph or a self-righteous satisfaction at the thought of putting them in their place, we need to back way off—immediately. But if our heart is breaking for them, if we truly want what's best for them, and if (after earnestly praying and seeking God for his direction) we feel absolutely convicted that this is a truth that must be spoken—at this very time and in this very place—then we proceed with holy boldness. With kindness and with compassion. Because sometimes speaking the truth is the most loving thing we can do (John 8:32).

"Appreciation can make a day, even change a life. Your willingness to put it into words is all that is necessary." —Margaret Cousins

Earnest Compliments and Heartfelt Appreciation. When was the last time we let the people around us know how much we love them, how much we value them and appreciate what they contribute to our lives and the lives of others? No doubt most of them are well aware of their faults and failings—but how about their strengths, their accomplishments and successes, their unique gifts and talents? We know how much it means to us when we're feeling discouraged, worn out, and "weary in well-doing" and out of the blue, someone compliments us or thanks us or lets us know our efforts haven't gone unnoticed. How it lifts our spirits and brightens our day! We need to get in the habit of doing the same for others, taking time—making time—every day.

I once attended a workshop at a teachers' conference entitled "Catch 'Em Doing Good." The speaker's premise was that instead of keeping an eye out for bad behavior, constantly calling our kids on the carpet, we should be looking for good behavior and rewarding cheerful obedience, acts of kindness and generosity, and good manners on display. She insisted it was a much more effective strategy for classroom discipline. The speaker promised that our children would be much more motivated by praise and positive reinforcement than the negative attention they received for misbehaving. When I got back to my classroom, I decided to give it a try—and I have to tell you, the change in their behavior and attitude was amazing—as was mine!

Perhaps you've heard the true story of another teacher who once asked her junior high students to write down one thing they admired or appreciated about each and every other student in the class. Later, she compiled the comments and gave all the students a list of the things their peers admired about them. For many of those students, it was a defining moment, a life-changing experience. Years and years later, when one of them died in Vietnam, the tattered old list was found in his wallet—it was among his most prized possessions.

Think about it: Who are the people in your life—in your family, in your church, in your school or office, in your neighborhood or community—who could use a sincere compliment or an expression of heartfelt appreciation from you?

Humor That Lightens the Load. The Bible says, "A cheerful heart is good medicine . . ." (Prov. 17:22). Many thousands of years and hundreds of research studies later, doctors and scientists agree! There is healing power in positive, uplifting humor. Somehow laughter relieves stress and releases tension; it helps us relax and unwind. When we can laugh at ourselves and with others, we can let go of a host of unhealthy emotions. A little silliness goes a long way to lessen the symptoms of physical, emotional, and psychological pain. Some women have a real flair for it, a comedic gift! But all of us can learn to use a little levity now and then to lighten someone else's load.

Exhortation and Encouragement. All of us have people in our lives who need to hear that we see their God-given potential, that we believe in them. We have the greatest expectations for what God will accomplish in them and through them. Sometimes we may even see in them things that they don't. But once they catch a glimpse, our faith in them becomes what motivates and inspires them, what propels them onward and upward until they become all that they were meant to be. It's our privilege to cheer them on every step of the way, challenging them to "dream big and work hard." When they run into obstacles or run out of gas, we can be the voice that says, "Don't give up. You can do it! I know you can! God is with you. He will help you. And so will I."

Compassion and Understanding. This is the opposite of criticism and condemnation. It's where we extend to others the mercy and grace that we have received. We let them know that they are not alone; there is someone who sees, someone who cares, someone who understands what they're going through. Our struggles may or may not be similar to theirs, but we know what it is to feel lonely, rejected, betrayed. We've made our own share of mistakes. We know how it feels to fall and fail. We also know where to find the strength to get back up again, to learn to love and trust and try again. So we point them in that direction. And we pray for them. Better yet, we pray *with* them.

I watched a news conference held by a man who had just lost everything—his wife, his two infant daughters, and his mother-in-law—when a military jet crashed into their home days before Christmas. With tears streaming down his face, the man expressed his deep concern *for the pilot* who had escaped unharmed, knowing he must be devastated by what he had done. The man asked everyone listening to pray for the pilot: "I want him to know that I don't blame him. It wasn't his fault. He didn't mean to do it. I want him to find peace." What an incredible gift this man gave to that pilot. It's the kind of Christlike compassion and understanding we all are called to. Still, seeing it lived out before us takes our breath away.

A Listening Ear. What do you say to a person who's just lost her job or home, a child or a spouse? To someone who's suffering physically, emotionally, mentally, or spiritually? Romans 12:15 tells us to mourn with those who mourn. We are to comfort them with our presence and our love. Let God use our arms to hold them, our ears to listen. "Praise be to the God and Father of our Lord Jesus Christ, the Father of compassion and the God of all comfort, who comforts us in all our troubles, so that we can comfort those in any trouble with the comfort we ourselves have received from God" (2 Cor. 1:3–4).

> "For beautiful eyes, look for the good in others; for beautiful lips, speak only words of kindness; and for poise, walk with the knowledge that you are never alone." —Audrey Hepburn

Sometimes we're in too much of a hurry to try to "fix" things and make them better. It's a trap I've fallen into. Many times I've caught myself trying to solve friends' problems by offering what I intend to be helpful suggestions. "Have you thought of this? Have you tried that? Maybe if you just. . . ." Often they will shoot down one idea after another. They have a million reasons why nothing I tell them will work. And still I keep trying, instead of getting the message: "I need your sympathy, not your solutions. A listening ear, not a list of things to do." I don't know why I'm so slow to pick up on this—especially considering how frustrating I find it when other people do it to me. I guess I really do just want to help, the same way others just want to help me. But years ago, I learned to tell my friends and family up front, "I may ask you for advice about this later; right now I just need you to listen." Now when they confide in me, I try to remember to ask them, "How can I help you with this? Are you looking for a sounding board? Do you want my suggestions? Or are you looking for a shoulder to cry on? Whatever you need, it's yours."

These are just a few of the powerful weapons available to us in the fight between good and evil that rages all around us. There are so many ways our words can be used to bring help and healing. We may never know this side of eternity the impact they have had in the lives of those we've touched—though sometimes God gives us a little glimpse, a sneak peek. It's such an awesome privilege to be his vessel, his voice. To speak his life, his love, his joy, his peace into someone else's heart.

And in one sense, it's so simple, so easy. Anyone can do it. Anytime. Any place.

Then again, it can be the challenge of a lifetime to tame the tongue, to harness this great power, and to learn to consistently wield it for good. It can take tremendous dedication and enormous effort on our part to resist the temptation of our selfish inclination, to overcome our human weakness, and to live up to the potential we've been given. Frankly, on our own, it's impossible. We need the Spirit of God himself to help us. And not just with the words that come tripping off our tongues—but with the source of those words: our hearts.

Bible Study

1. Can you think of a time in your life when someone else's words have encouraged you or comforted you or built you up? It might have been a moment when a compliment, an expression of love or appreciation, or maybe just some good, practical, down-to-earth advice made all the difference?

   a. Take a moment now to thank God for these people and their ministry to you.

   b. Have you ever thanked any of these people personally? Do they know what they did for you? If it's appropriate, consider how you might express your appreciation to them today.

2. To your knowledge, have you ever had the opportunity to speak powerful, positive, life-giving words to someone else's heart? Were you aware of it at the time? Did you sense God leading you to say what you said? Or did you find out later that it was particularly meaningful to the other person?

3. Read Romans 12:9–21. According to this passage, what should our attitude be toward:

   a. God and spiritual things (11–12)?

   b. God's people—our brothers and sisters in Christ (10, 13, 15)?

   c. Those who persecute us and mistreat us (14, 17–21)?

   d. Life in general (9, 12, 16, 18, 21)?

How does having this kind of attitude affect the words we choose to speak—to God, to God's people, to those who persecute and mistreat us, or just in general?

4. Make a list of people you will take time to encourage this week—friends and neighbors, coworkers, your husband, your children or grandchildren, brothers and sisters, or brothers and sisters in Christ. Ask God if there's anyone special he'd like you to include

on that list. Be open to any and every opportunity! Consider which of these expressions might be the most appropriate and/or meaningful, given the circumstances:

- ☐ On-the-spot, in the moment, verbal expressions of praise or admiration
- ☐ Handwritten letters, notes, postcards
- ☐ E-mail or e-cards
- ☐ Awards or certificates of recognition
- ☐ Fellowship over coffee or a meal or during a special activity
- ☐ Phone calls
- ☐ Posts on a Web site/blog/message board
- ☐ Love notes left in lunchboxes or on pillows

5. Choose one of the following verses or (one mentioned previously) to memorize and meditate on this week:

Proverbs 10:11a	Proverbs 15:4
Proverbs 10:21a	Proverbs 15:23
Proverbs 10:31a	Proverbs 16:21
Proverbs 12:14	Proverbs 25:11
Proverbs 12:25	

6. Take a few moments to record any further thoughts or reflections.

Four

Words That Reveal

"Search me, O God, and know my heart. . . ."
(Ps. 139:23)

In our time, many know her as the first American poet and one of the most important figures in American literature. In her time, she was simply Mrs. Bradstreet—the wife of Governor Simon Bradstreet of the Massachusetts Bay Colony and the mother of their eight children. Anne was sixteen when she married Simon. They were Puritans. Together with their friends and family, they had fled to the New World to escape the religious persecution they had experienced in England. Thousands of miles across the ocean, far away from everything they knew and loved, they had begun rebuilding their lives under the harshest of conditions, in the most difficult circumstances. Daily they were confronted with sickness and suffering and death. Anne especially desperately missed her homeland and the life she once knew. Still, she realized that she was blessed. She was deeply in love with her husband, and he with her. They both came from families that were better off than most. At a time when few women received any formal education (it wasn't necessary for the kind of lives they were expected to lead), both Anne's father and husband encouraged her to explore her interest in history and philosophy, language, literature, theology, the arts, and the sciences. She was fluent in three or four languages. In those days, most homes could boast only one book (if that)—the Bible. The books in Anne's personal library eventually numbered over eight hundred, each and every one a prized possession. They inspired her to try her own hand at writing. Though in the 1600s there was little market for poetry written by a woman, her family celebrated and applauded her efforts.

"The people and circumstances around me do not make me what I am, they reveal who I am." —Laura Schlessinger

Then on July 10, 1666, tragedy struck. In the middle of the night the Bradstreet home caught fire and burned to the ground. Thankfully, the family escaped unharmed. But they could only stand there and watch as all of their precious belongings— everything they owned—went up in smoke. It was a devastating loss. Later, Anne poured out her feelings in a poem she titled "Upon the Burning of Our House":

In silent night when rest I took,
For sorrow near I did not look,
I waken'd was with thund'ring noise
And piteous shrieks of dreadful voice.
That fearful sound of "Fire" and "Fire,"
Let no man know is my desire.
I starting up, the light did spy,
And to my God my heart did cry
To straighten me in my distress

And not to leave me succor-less.
Then coming out, behold a space
The flame consume my dwelling place.

And when I could no longer look,
I blest His grace that gave and took,
That laid my goods now in the dust.
Yea, so it was, and so 'twas just.
It was His own; it was not mine.
Far be it that I should repine,
He might of all justly bereft
But yet sufficient for us left.

When by the ruins oft I past
My sorrowing eyes aside did cast
And here and there the places spy
Where oft I sat and long did lie.
Here stood that trunk, and there that chest,
There lay that store I counted best,
My pleasant things in ashes lie,
And them behold no more shall I.
Under the roof no guest shall sit,
Nor at thy table eat a bit.
No pleasant talk shall 'ere be told
Nor things recounted done of old.
No candle 'ere shall shine in thee,
Nor bridegroom's voice 'ere heard shall be.
In silence ever shalt thou lie.
Adieu, adieu, all's vanity.

Then straight I 'gan my heart to chide:
And did thy wealth on earth abide,
Didst fix thy hope on moldering dust,
The arm of flesh didst make thy trust?
Raise up thy thoughts above the sky
That dunghill mists away may fly.
Thou hast a house on high erect
Fram'd by that mighty Architect,
With glory richly furnished

Stands permanent, though this be fled.
It's purchased, and paid for, too,
By Him who hath enough to do.
A price so vast as is unknown,
Yet by His gift is made thine own.
There's wealth enough; I need no more.
Farewell, my pelf; farewell, my store.
The world no longer let me love;
My hope and treasure lies above.[1]

It was a defining moment for Anne. A real-life, honest-to-goodness, flesh-and-blood woman, she wrestled with grief and sorrow and self-pity. But in the end, the words that came pouring out of her heart were words of hope and faith and peace and trust. Words of praise and thanksgiving to God.[2] Anne's response to this heartbreaking loss tells us far more about her than any biographer ever could. Jesus said: "Out of the abundance of the heart, the mouth speaks" (Matt. 12:34, ESV).

Our words are a reflection and a revelation of who we are inside. They reveal our focus and our frame of mind—where we really are emotionally and spiritually. As Jesus explained to his disciples, "The things that come out of the mouth come from the heart . . ." (Matt. 15:18). "The good man brings good things out of the good stored up in his heart, and the evil man brings evil things out of the evil stored up in his heart. For out of the overflow of his heart his mouth speaks" (Luke 6:45).

"Words, like nature, half reveal
and half conceal the soul within."
—Lord Alfred Tennyson

For good or bad, for better or worse, our words reveal what's in our hearts—because that's where they begin. They are signs or "symptoms" of our heart's condition. If our hearts are tender, merciful, and compassionate, our words will show it. If we've been nurturing the fruit of the Spirit (love, joy, peace, patience, kindness, goodness, faithfulness, gentleness, and self-control, Gal. 5:22–23), that fruit will be evident in the things we say as well as the things we do. Conversely, if our hearts are self-centered and self-focused, if they are hard and callused, if they are bitter or greedy or envious or proud, our words will reveal that, too.

> "Be careful of your thoughts;
> they may become words at any
> moment." —Iara Gassen

Did I say that out loud? We may be able to keep up appearances for a while. Some of us have become experts at camouflaging our true intentions, presenting our thoughts and opinions and motives in the best possible light. But taming the tongue is tricky. Sooner or later, the truth always slips out. When the cameras are turned off and the lights have gone dark, when we think no one's listening—no one important, that is—our mouths tell what we *really* think. If only to ourselves.

Think about it. If our words are constantly angry or impatient, hurtful or insensitive, what does that say about us? What if our words are manipulative and controlling—if we're convinced we know better or we're always trying to get our own way? What if we can't stop talking about how much we have and how much it cost and how exclusive it is? If we've got to be the center of attention, the focal point of every conversation? If we have to one-up every story we hear to show that we have more experience, more knowledge, more everything? If we feel compelled to criticize others and pass judgment on them—behind their backs or to their faces? If we habitually undermine those in authority over us? If we relish playing the devil's advocate? If "contrary" or "argumentative" is our automatic pre-set?

Sometimes the root of it all is selfishness. Sometimes it's fear. Doubt. Insecurity. Disappointment or disillusionment. Bitterness. Pride. Whatever the cause, it eventually finds its expression in a way that not only hurts us, but others. It may be a slow, quiet, insidious poison or a volcanic eruption. Either way, the damage is undeniable—and sometimes irreversible.

We can resolve all we want to get a tighter rein on our tongues, to set a guard over our lips, to refuse to utter words that wound and instead choose words that heal. But if words begin in our hearts, it doesn't do any good to try to treat the symptoms and ignore the disease. We need to schedule an appointment with the Great Physician, ask him about our heart condition, and get his diagnosis and prescription. We may have an idea of what's wrong with us, what the signs and symptoms are pointing to. We may think we know what areas we need to work on or improve (the spiritual equivalent of diet and exercise). But only God knows for sure. Only he is qualified to make the diagnosis.

"The heart is hopelessly dark and deceitful, a puzzle that no one can figure out. But I, God, search the heart and examine the mind. I get to the heart of the human. I get to the root of things. I treat them as they really are, not as they pretend to be" (Jer. 17:9–10, MESSAGE). We may be able to fool some of the people some of the time. We may even fool ourselves. But nothing gets past the Lord. "Nothing in all creation is hidden from God's sight. Everything is uncovered and laid bare before the eyes of him to whom we must give account" (Heb. 4:13).

It's uncomfortable to be exposed. To have all of our deepest, darkest secrets brought to light. To find out that we're only human after all, as weak and frail and fallen as everyone else. We may be shocked and horrified. We may feel embarrassed or ashamed. But God isn't shocked or horrified. It's nothing new to him, nothing he didn't already know. There is nothing he hasn't seen. The amazing, incredible, wonderful, fabulous news is that he loves us anyway—just as we are. But he loves us far too much to leave us that way. He knows the pain and suffering our own sinfulness causes us, and he wants to do something about it. He's willing to take drastic measures to set us free.

Can love be terrible, my Lord?
    Can gentleness be stern?
Ah yes!—intense is love's desire
To purify his loved—'tis fire,
    A holy fire to burn.
For he must fully perfect thee
Till in thy likeness all may see
    The beauty of thy Lord.

Can holy love be jealous, Lord?
    Yes jealous as the grave;
Till every hurtful idol be
Uptorn and wrested out of thee
    Love will be stern to save;
Will spare thee not a single pain
Till thou be freed and pure again
    And perfect as thy Lord.

Can love seem cruel, O my Lord?
    Yes, like a sword the cure;
He will not spare thee, sin-sick soul,
Till he hath made thy sickness whole,
    Until thine heart is pure.
For oh! He loves thee far too well
To leave thee in thy self-made hell,
    A Savior is thy Lord![3]

If we'll humble ourselves, if we'll submit ourselves to God's surgical intervention, he will cleanse us completely. He'll clean out those clogged arteries and scrape off the calluses and cut through the scar tissue. He'll even give us a complete transplant, if necessary (if we haven't already had one), leaving us with a brand-new heart. And a fresh start.

For the full benefit, we have to regularly schedule follow-up appointments to make sure our new heart is beating properly, that it's healing as it should and growing stronger day by day. And we have to follow the Doctor's instructions for post-op care: "Above all else, guard your heart, for it is the wellspring of life" (Prov. 4:23).

Someone once observed that the human heart is like a bucket. Whenever it's "bumped," it spills what's inside. It's simple, really: If we want good things to come spilling out, we have to put good things in. We have to fill our buckets (our hearts) with things that are positive, encouraging, and spiritually uplifting. Meditate on the Word of God. Spend time in praise and worship and thanksgiving, and in the company of others who share our commitment to good "heart" health. "Finally, brothers, whatever is true, whatever is noble, whatever is right, whatever is pure, whatever is lovely, whatever is admirable—if anything is excellent or praiseworthy—think about such things" (Phil. 4:8).

We can't just put good things in; we have to keep bad things out. We've got to limit or eliminate junk food, get rid of the unhealthy or negative influences. They may be internal—thoughts we dwell on, feelings we wallow in. Or they may be external: things we read and watch and listen to that only feed our greed or envy or lust, our dissatisfaction or disappointment with life. Things that tempt us to compare ourselves or our family members unfavorably to others. Things that convince us we belong in the center of the universe and that we have a right to demand our own way. Things that depress and discourage us. Sometimes there are specific people we need to limit our time with or certain places we need to avoid. It can be difficult to disentangle ourselves from our old habits, our old routine, and our old way of life. But it's not as difficult as going through the surgery again. We don't want to undo all the work God has done.

Today the word "Pollyanna" is often used as a derogatory term for someone who is naively optimistic, intentionally blind to unpleasant truths, or willfully, woefully out of touch with the harsh realities of life. But if you've ever read the original novel by Eleanor H. Porter or seen the Disney movie version featuring Hayley Mills, you know better. Porter's Pollyanna is a little girl whose minister-father taught her from an early age to cultivate in her heart "an attitude of gratitude"—to choose to "give thanks in all circumstances" (1 Thess. 5:18). Together, they played "the glad game," in which they tried to help each other find something to be glad or grateful for, no matter what the situation. Pollyanna's father also taught her an important lesson he had learned the hard way: to always look for the good in others, rather than focus on their faults and flaws.

> "Your mind is a garden, your thoughts
> are the seeds; the harvest can either be
> flowers or weeds." —Author Unknown

As the story unfolds, the young girl experiences more than her share of heartache. When her beloved parents die, she's sent to live with a wealthy aunt—a cold and distant woman who dominates the social structure of an unhappy, unfriendly town. But Pollyanna's spirit will not be stifled or subdued. She looks for the good in everyone and everything—and finds it! Her enthusiasm is so contagious, it spreads to from one person to another. Even her hard-hearted aunt can't help but soften in response to Pollyanna's steadfast determination to rejoice and be glad. At the end of the story, when Pollyanna faces a loss that for once threatens to overwhelm even her resolutely cheerful spirit, the townspeople rally around her. One by one they repeat to her the very words that she herself has said to them, words of love and friendship, faith and hope. Words that have forever changed them. Words that have come from a pure heart, a thankful heart, a happy heart. It's a powerful illustration of a profound spiritual truth: When our hearts are full of life and grace, our words will be, too—a true reflection, a revelation of the One we live to serve.

Bible Study

1. Think about the words you speak on a daily basis. Ask the Holy Spirit to shine the light of his truth as you consider: How well do your words reflect your heart? For better or worse, what do your words reveal about you—to yourself and others? What is your heart's condition?

2. Do you see some areas where (perhaps over the years) there's been real spiritual growth or improvement? Are there signs or "symptoms" that indicate there are other areas that now need your attention? How urgent is the need—and why?

3. Read David's prayer of confession and repentance in Psalm 51.

   a. What does David ask God to do for him and his sinful heart? What action does he ask God to take (1–2, 7, 9–10, 12)?

   b. What does God want to see in our hearts (6)? As opposed to what?

   c. What does God want from us, in return for what he does for us (16–17)?

    d. When our hearts are cleansed and made new—
       and filled with God's truth—what kind of words
       come out of our mouths (13–15)?

4. Write your own prayer of confession and repentance.

5. Has God impressed on your heart any specific action you need to take in response to what he has revealed about your heart's condition? Take some time to think about this.

6. What can you start doing today to fill your heart with good things?

7. Are there certain things or people or circumstances you need to avoid? How can you keep negative influences at bay?

8. Is there someone you can ask to hold you accountable and help you keep your commitment to make these changes?

9. Choose one of the following verses (or one mentioned previously) to memorize and meditate on this week.

Psalm 51:10–12	Galatians 5:22–23
Psalm 119:11	Philippians 4:8
Proverbs 4:23	Colossians 3:1–2
Proverbs 16:23	Colossians 3:15–17
Ezekiel 36:26–27	

10. Record any further thoughts or reflections.

Five

Words That Live

"For the word of God is living and active. Sharper than any double-edged sword, it penetrates even to dividing soul and spirit. . . ." (Heb. 4:12)

"**Don't** let it end like this. Tell them I said something!"

These are the dying words of Mexican revolutionary Pancho Villa. It would almost be funny, if it weren't so sad. There he lay, bleeding to death of a gunshot wound, the victim of an assassination attempt by one of his many enemies. Reviled as a villain by some, hailed as a hero by others, he wanted to say something profound that would live up to the legend and the legacy he had tried to create. He wanted to utter some incredibly wise or insightful words that would live on forever. Only he couldn't think of anything. He didn't have time. Neither did England's Queen Elizabeth I. With her last breath, she exclaimed: "All my possessions for a moment of time!"

Our imprint on time and space, our place in human history is only temporary. As the prophet Isaiah said, "All men are like grass, and all their glory is like the flowers of the field. The grass withers and the flowers fall . . ." (Isa. 40:6–7). No matter how prestigious our position in life, no matter how impressive our accomplishments, no matter how profound and memorable our words, they will one day fade into oblivion—completely and utterly forgotten. "But the word of the Lord stands forever" (1 Pet. 1:24–25).

God's Word alone is eternal and everlasting. Only those words that find their source in his will live on through the ages.

For generations, many scientists and philosophers and theologians have observed that on the most basic level, what separates us as human beings from the animal kingdom is our ability to speak. We don't just communicate primal emotion or information necessary for survival (which we now know animals do), but we express abstract thoughts and ideas, tell stories, share memories, and encourage or inspire or persuade. The ability to speak—to communicate with words—is one of the most significant ways in which we reflect our heritage, our parentage; we are created "in the image of God."

> "I believe the Bible is the best gift God has ever given to man. All the good from the Savior of the world is communicated to us through this book." —Abraham Lincoln

The book of Genesis tells us that when God created the world, he spoke it into existence. "And God said, 'Let there be light,' and there was light." Presumably he could have done it any number of other ways, but for some specific reason he chose to speak. He chose to use words to bring the world to life. He chose to use *the* Word.

The gospel of John tells us, "In the beginning was the Word, and the Word was with God, and the Word was God. He was with God in the beginning. Through him all things were made; without him nothing was made that has been made. . . . He was in the world, and though the world was made through him, the world did not recognize him. He came to that which was his own, but his own did not receive him. Yet to all who received him, to those who believed in his name, he gave the right to become children of God . . ." (John 1:1–3, 10–12). John explains that Jesus is the Word of which he speaks. "The Word became flesh and made his dwelling among us. We have seen his glory, the glory of the One and Only, who came from the Father, full of grace and truth" (John 1:14).

Not only is Jesus the living embodiment of the Word of God, the Word of Life, the Word of Truth, but he proclaims this Word—this message from above: "The words I have spoken to you are spirit and they are life" (John 6:63).

John goes on to tell us of a time when Jesus offered this life to a Samaritan woman; the encounter forever changed her and impacted her whole community in a lasting way: "Now he had to go through Samaria . . . and Jesus, tired as he was from the journey, sat down by the well. It was about the sixth hour" (John 4:4, 6). Bible scholars explain that to say Jesus "had to go" through Samaria is remarkable, because in those days, Jews did not *have* to go into or through Samaria to get anywhere they were going. They very deliberately went around it. But apparently Jesus had a divine appointment. There was someone he went there to meet.

"When a Samaritan woman came to draw water, Jesus said to her, 'Will you give me a drink?'. . . The Samaritan woman said to him, 'You are a Jew and I am a Samaritan woman. How can you ask me for a drink?' (For Jews do not associate with Samaritans.)" (John 4:7, 9). That wasn't the only thing that made his request unusual. Even among those who did not count themselves as his disciples, Jesus was widely respected as a rabbi—a religious teacher and a moral authority. To engage a woman in conversation alone, one-on-one, was highly questionable behavior. And such a woman! As the subheadings in many Bibles note, this was a "much-married" woman. That she'd been to the altar with most of her lovers did nothing to minimize the fact that she'd had many. By choosing to come to the well in the heat of the day, instead of the customary time (early morning or late evening), she may have been purposely avoiding unpleasant interaction with the other women of the village. No doubt she was used to being the subject of much gossip and derision. But Jesus looked past all of that. He said to her: "If you knew the gift of God and who it is that asks you for a drink, you would have asked him and he would have given you living water" (John 4:10).

This answer mystified her.

"Sir," the woman said, "You have nothing to draw with and the well is deep. Where can you get this living water? . . ."

Jesus answered, "Everyone who drinks this water will be thirsty again, but whoever drinks the water I give him will never thirst. Indeed, the water I give him will become in him a spring of water welling up to eternal life."

The woman said to him, "Sir, give me this water so that I won't get thirsty and have to keep coming here to draw water."

He told her, "Go, call your husband and come back."

"I have no husband," she replied.

Jesus said to her, "You are right when you say you have no husband. The fact is, you have had five husbands, and the man you now have is not your husband. What you have just said is quite true." (John 4:11, 13–18)

Stunned that a stranger could be familiar with the intimate details of her personal life, she exclaimed: "Sir . . . I can see that you are a prophet" (v. 19). She tried to deflect the attention and take the conversation in a different direction. She asked him about the doctrinal issue at the crux of the division between Samaritans and Jews, but she didn't fully understand his answer. So she concluded: "'I know that Messiah' (called Christ) 'is coming. When he comes, he will explain everything to us.' Then Jesus declared, 'I who speak to you am he'" (John 4:25–26).

It was a mind-boggling, earth-shattering moment. Could she possibly be standing face to face with the One whose coming had been so looked for and longed for—for thousands of years?

This was not something she could keep to herself. She ran all the way back to town, calling out, "Come, see a man who told me everything I ever did. Could this be the Christ?" (v. 29).

> "Every day we live is a priceless gift of God, loaded with possibilities to learn something new, to gain fresh insights into His great truths." —Dale Evans Rogers

Scripture tells us: "Many of the Samaritans from that town believed in him because of the woman's testimony, 'He told me everything I ever did.' . . . And because of his words many more became believers. They said to the woman, 'We no longer believe just because of what you said; now we have heard for ourselves, and we know that this man really is the Savior of the world'" (John 4:39, 41–42).

Just now, reading over this passage of Scripture, I find my eyes welling up with tears. Imagine being the woman at the well. Just standing there, talking with Jesus. Hearing him reveal to you something so precious, so powerful, so transforming, so all-consuming. The world would never, ever be the same. Centuries of wise men, scholars and theologians, and prophets and kings would have given their lives to witness and experience the moment when Jesus said, "I who speak to you am he."

I wish I could have been there. Maybe you do, too. But the reality is that we have something the woman at the well didn't have: the opportunity to encounter Jesus every day through the pages of his Word. Every time we open our Bibles, we can hear him speak. It's how we get to know him, how we learn to relate to him personally and intimately, and how we grow to become the people he has meant for us to be.

The apostle Paul explained, "All Scripture is God-breathed and is useful for teaching, rebuking, correcting and training in righteousness, so that the man of God may be thoroughly equipped for every good work" (2 Tim. 3:16–17). The psalmist said, "Your word is a lamp to my feet and a light for my path" (Ps. 119:105).

The Bible is also a mirror: when we look into it, we see ourselves more clearly. We discover how close or how far we are from the standards God has for us. It's so easy to compare ourselves to others in a way that makes us feel comfortable and complacent. We can rationalize or minimize nearly all of our faults and failings, if only we compare ourselves to the right person or people. But the mirror doesn't lie. It shows us exactly who we are, exactly how God views our thoughts and attitudes and behaviors, exactly how we compare to *him*. Sometimes it's painful—excruciatingly so. But it's far better to find out what's wrong and have the opportunity to fix it than to go on living a life that's a tragic mess. Making the same mistakes over and over again, falling into the same traps. Failing to live up to even a fraction of our potential. Missing the chance to experience forgiveness and restoration, spiritual growth and maturity. Most of us spend hours fussing over our outward, physical appearance. Even on the busiest of mornings, in the craziest rush, we pause for at least a cursory glance in the mirror before we head out the door. How can the source of our true beauty—our inner woman, our spiritual self—be any less important?

Hebrews 4:12 says, "For the word of God is living and active. Sharper than any double-edged sword, it penetrates even to dividing soul and spirit. . . ." The Bible is our measure. Unbiased and objective, it helps us determine whether our words are good and right and true, whether they're kind and helpful and uplifting—or not. So the question is never, "Are my words wiser or kinder than hers? Do I treat my kids, my husband, coworkers, or friends better than she does? Better than 'most'?" It's: "How do my words line up with God's? Are they what he says they should be?"

The Bible is our material source for all the things that—in our heart of hearts—we want our words to be: comfort, strength, wisdom, guidance, instruction, inspiration, encouragement, and blessing. It's where we go to fill up our "bucket" with good things, so that good things come spilling out.

Jesus said, "If you live in Me [abide vitally united to Me] and My words remain in you and continue to live in your hearts, ask whatever you will, and it shall be done for you. When you bear (produce) much fruit, My Father is honored and glorified, and you show and prove yourselves to be true followers of Mine" (John 15:7–8, AMPLIFIED).

"Nobody ever outgrows Scripture; the book widens and deepens with our years." —Charles Haddon Spurgeon

Maybe we spend a couple of minutes rehearsing a Scripture on a sticky note attached to the bathroom mirror or reflecting on the verse-for-the-day on our desk calendar or one that was e-mailed to us. We might read through a five- or ten- or fifteen-minute devotional, settle into our favorite chair for an extended Bible study and prayer time, or listen to an audio version of the Scriptures in the car or on the treadmill. Perhaps we regularly attend a Sunday school class, small group Bible study, or women's retreat. We may even sign up for a course at a local Christian college or university. There are a hundred and one ways to see that the Word of life lives in us. We just have to be convinced that it's truly worth what is sometimes a real sacrifice of our time and effort. We've got to be committed.

I want to be like the psalmist who said, "I will study your commandments and reflect on your ways. I will delight in your decrees and not forget your word" (Ps. 119:15–16, NLT*)*. But it's a constant struggle. There are seasons of my life when I'm very consistent, when I never miss a day, when I feel like I'm growing in leaps and bounds, learning so much. I can't get enough! Then there are dry or "desert" seasons, when I feel like I'm just going through the motions, determined to stick with it only because I know it's such a vital spiritual discipline. And as Elisabeth Elliot once said: "I don't pray when I'm in the mood any more than I wash dishes when I'm in the mood . . . pray 'til you feel like praying!" If I press on and persevere, I know that "times of refreshing" will come again (Acts 3:19). And then there are seasons when I let it all fall by the wayside. I get too busy, too distracted, too discouraged, or frankly, too rebellious. I don't feel like being confronted with my spiritual apathy or my bad attitude. I don't particularly want to look in the mirror—any more than I want to step on the scale!

> "Whatever need or trouble you are in, there is always something to help you in your Bible, if only you go on reading 'til you come to the word God specially has for you. . . . Sometimes the special word is in the portion you would naturally read, or in the Psalm for the day . . . but you must go on 'til you find it, for it is always somewhere. You will know it the moment you come to it, for it will rest your heart." —Amy Carmichael

During one such time a few years ago, I had lunch with a dear friend who had just returned from a short-term missions trip in Latin America. She had many deeply moving stories to tell about the desperation of the people she ministered to—the poverty, the sickness, the starvation. She told of the gratitude with which they received even the simplest kindness, the smallest gift. But what caught my attention most was her description of the local village pastors she had met, not one of whom owned even a single Bible. A few had proudly produced plastic sandwich bags in which they had carefully preserved a handful of pages torn from a worn-out old Bible divided among them—perhaps a few psalms or a New Testament book or two. They were only too happy to have these accidental excerpts and to live in a country where it wasn't illegal to own them. The wrinkled scraps of paper were their most prized possession. With the few Scriptures they had in those little plastic bags, they were teaching and training and discipling their congregations, evangelizing and counseling members of the community.

I thought of all the Bibles crowding my shelves at home: my first Bible—a children's Bible with old-fashioned illustrations—that my great-grandmother had given me for my fifth birthday; *The Student Bible* I bought with my babysitting money when I was a teenager, and the one I bought to replace it when it fell apart; *The Women's Devotional Bible* with flowery pink borders and sidebars featuring quotes and anecdotes from my favorite women authors; *The Parallel Bible* and the *Chain Reference Bible* and the study Bibles in different translations that I got when I decided I wanted to do some "serious" in-depth study. The *One-Year Bible*, the *Two-Year Bible*, the *90-Day Bible*, *The Chronological Bible*; Bibles they were giving away at banquets and conventions I attended; Bibles to accompany specific study methods, groups, or courses. Then there were the beautiful little Bibles I had acquired more recently, in a variety of colors and designs—accessories like shoes or earrings to go with different outfits (or perhaps, more accurately, purchased for the same reason I buy a dress in the size I hope to be when I reach my goal weight, as motivation, inspiration, incentive). Maybe the color of one of these Bibles, the unique design, or the soft feel of the leather would somehow entice me to pick it up and read it more often.

Out of curiosity, I decided to count them all. I discovered I owned more than thirty Bibles—most of them covered with dust, sitting unopened on my shelf or nightstand. I thought of those precious Latin American pastors and their counterparts all over the world. And in that moment, I could not have been more ashamed. Or convicted.

How many times in my life have I been desperate for wisdom and guidance, longing for love and comfort and peace and hope? How often have I wanted to be a better woman, to have more impact—more *positive* impact—on the lives of those around me? In my efforts, I've gone searching everywhere but the Scriptures, running to anyone or anything *but* God, the Author of life itself—the Source of all wisdom and knowledge and truth.

All too often I've gone hungry and thirsty, when the Bread of Heaven—the Living Water—the eternal, life-giving Word of God was right there in front of me, waiting for me:

Like the woman at the well, I was seeking
　For things that could not satisfy.
And then I heard my Savior speaking:
　"Draw from My well that never shall run dry."

Fill my cup, Lord, I lift it up, Lord!
　Come and quench this thirsting of my soul;
Bread of Heaven, feed me 'til I want no more.
　Fill my cup, fill it up and make me whole!

Bible Study

1. If you knew you were about to die, and you had the chance to say one last thing to your friends and family (or to the world itself), what would it be?

FILL MY CUP, LORD, Richard Blanchard, (c) 1959 Word Music, LLC. All Rights Reserved. Used By Permission.

2. Read Jeremiah 2:13. Through the prophet Jeremiah, God confronted his people and held them accountable for two sins that were particularly offensive—an affront or insult—to him. What were they?

3. Have you ever been guilty of these sins? Where do you usually turn for wisdom, guidance, encouragement, comfort, and strength? When the going gets tough, who or what do you run to?

4. Now read the invitation God issues in Isaiah 55.

   a. Who is invited (1)?

   b. What is God offering (1–3)?

   c. What is the cost (1)?

   d. What kind of response is required? How do we RSVP? Look for action words (1–3, 6–7).

   e. What does God compare his Word to? What does he promise it will do (10–11)?

5. Choose one of the following verses (or one mentioned previously in the chapter) to memorize and meditate on this week.

   Matthew 4:4   Colossians 3:16

   John 6:67–68   2 Timothy 2:15

   Romans 10:17   Hebrews 4:12

6. Take a few moments to record any further thoughts or reflections.

Six

Words That Die

"Truthful lips endure forever, but a lying tongue lasts only a moment." (Prov. 12:19)

Just as there are words that live, there are words that die—or words that should die, long before they ever come tripping off our tongues. Like words that live, words that die have power. Destructive, devastating, deadly power. Especially to the spirits of those who speak them. This I know from painful personal experience.

As a young woman, I once suffered what felt like an unending series of bitter disappointments and heartaches. I watched my family suffer, too—physically, mentally, emotionally, spiritually, and financially. On and on and on our suffering went. I didn't know how much more we could take. I prayed faithfully and fervently for God to intervene and come to our rescue. But every time it seemed there was a light at the end of the tunnel, it turned out to be the headlight of an oncoming train. I believed for miracles that didn't happen. I prayed for provision and healing and deliverance that didn't come.

My theology was pretty solid. I understood the concept of the sovereignty of God, that he has the right to do as he sees fit, that when he says "no," it's always for a good reason, and that suffering tests our faith and builds our character and produces fruit that glorifies him. But after a while, I could no longer find any comfort in those truths. I felt I'd been pushed beyond the breaking point, beyond anything I could bear. I was hurt, I was angry, and I was bitter. And in my hurt and anger and bitterness, I lashed out at God. I started saying things to myself like, "Yes, God *could* do a miracle in this situation—but he *won't*. He *could* prevent this from happening, but he *doesn't want to*. He *could* provide for us, but he's *not going to*." Whenever a whisper of hope came to my heart, I slapped it away with a sarcastic remark.

If you'd asked me then, I would have told you that I was just being realistic, simply steeling myself against further disappointment. I was hardening my heart to protect it. But looking back, I see the ugly truth: I was trying to hurt God the way I felt he had hurt me.

I didn't mean anything I said. I didn't truly believe it. They were just idle words.

The Message translates Jesus' warning in Matthew 12:36 as "Let me tell you something: Every one of these careless words is going to come back to haunt you. There will be a time of Reckoning. Words are powerful; take them seriously. . . ."

For almost two years, I kept up this tantrum (have I mentioned that I was a strong-willed child?), kicking and screaming, insisting that my Father didn't love me, didn't care about me. But all the time deep down, I was desperately hoping he would prove me wrong. If I thought God had made my life miserable, it was nothing compared to the misery I created for myself. Life was just as hard or harder, only now I had nowhere to turn, no one to turn to.

Eventually the day came when I realized I couldn't stand it another minute. I knew I had to let go. I had to give in. I had to accept that God was God and could do whatever he wanted in my life, and that I was going to love him and serve him anyway. As Job said, "Though he slay me, yet will I trust in him . . ." (Job 13:15, KJV). Or as Peter said, when many of Jesus' disciples had abandoned him and Jesus asked if the Twelve were going to leave him, too: "Lord, to whom shall we go? You alone have the words of eternal life" (John 6:68, TLB).

"Words which do not give the light of Christ increase the darkness." —Mother Teresa

When it was all over, when I was all cried out and had calmed down and was ready to see sense, when I'd received his forgiveness and wanted to start fresh, I tried to take those first feeble steps of faith—only to be met with an internal recording made in my own voice, saying over and over again that God could not be trusted, that he would only disappoint me, abandon me, or forsake me. I had played it so many times, it was burned into my brain. And on some level I had come to believe it was true. Overcoming the deceit and discouragement of this internal voice required one of the longest, hardest spiritual battles I have ever fought. It took years to undo the damage. Even today I sometimes find vestiges of it hidden away in the corners of my heart, in the most unexpected places—coming out of nowhere to threaten all the progress I have made and take me back to that awful, awful place. I can't tell you how much I regret the things I said back then.

Scripture tells us there are words that should never cross our lips—words that not only wound others, but ourselves. Words that are poison to our spirits, our hearts, and our minds. Words that dishonor God and damage our witness. Words for which we will one day be called to account. James tell us, "If you claim to be religious but don't control your tongue, you are fooling yourself, and your religion is worthless" (James 1:26 NLT).

Lies, Half-Truths, and Exaggerations. The ninth commandment seems straightforward enough. Just four little words: "You shall not lie." Six, if you're using an older translation: "Thou shalt not bear false witness." But the Westminster Larger Catechism enumerates more than fifty different ways it's possible to break that commandment, to violate the spirit of it—the Spirit of Truth.[1] These sins are an affront to God because he is Truth. Anything less than "the God's honest truth" has no part in him. And if we are not in him, if we are not his—then who do we belong to?

Jesus told the dishonest and deceitful Pharisees, "You belong to your father, the devil. . . . He was a murderer from the beginning, not holding to the truth, for there is no truth in him. When he lies, he speaks his native language, for he is a liar and the father of lies" (John 8:44).

The beginning, of course, was the garden of Eden, where the father of lies approached "the mother of all living" (Eve) with what sounded like an innocent question. The serpent asked her, "Did God really say, 'You must not eat from any tree in the garden?'" (Gen. 3:1). But the serpent was crafty—more crafty than any of the creatures God had made. He skillfully drew the unsuspecting woman into a conversation that would have deadly consequences. Eve obligingly explained God's command (Bible scholars point out that she actually exaggerated or overstated it) and the punishment for eating from the tree of the knowledge of good and evil. But the serpent contradicted her. "You will not surely die," he hissed. "For God knows that when you eat of it, your eyes will be opened, and you will be like God, knowing good and evil" (Gen. 3:4–5). The serpent lied. Then Eve lied; then Adam lied. And Paradise was lost.

"Oh what a tangled web we weave, when first we practice to deceive."[2]

The trouble with lies (even little "white" ones) is that when we're caught in one, as we inevitably will be, it compromises our integrity, tarnishes our reputation, destroys the trust, and undermines the faith that others have in us—and in the God we claim we serve. Not only that, but one lie tends to lead to another and another. Soon enough we can lie without conscience, because we start to believe everything that comes out of our own mouth. We lose the ability to distinguish between the truth and a lie. And that is a very dangerous place to be.

"The LORD detests lying lips, but he delights in those who tell the truth" (Prov. 12:22, NLT). God wants us to be honest, first and foremost with him and with ourselves. "Surely you desire truth in the inner parts; you teach me wisdom in the inmost place" (Ps. 51:6). Then we can be honest with each other. You know, it is possible to be truthful *and* tactful. It is possible to be honest without being unnecessarily hurtful or unkind. God has called us to live a life of integrity, and he can give us the wisdom and strength to walk in it. He will teach us what to say.

Profanity and Obscenity. "But among you there must not be even a hint of sexual immorality, or of any kind of impurity, or of greed, because these are improper for God's holy people. Nor should there be obscenity, foolish talk or coarse joking, which are out of place, but rather thanksgiving" (Eph. 5:3–4). These days it's hard to imagine that there was a time when the fact that there were "ladies present" meant that certain words and subjects were off-limits in polite conversation. Today, "ladies" are some of the biggest offenders!

Some of us had a life "BC"—before Christ—in an environment in which profanity and obscenity weren't frowned upon, and we find it difficult to rid our vocabulary of certain words and phrases. Others of us never heard that kind of language in our own homes growing up, but it's become so commonplace in our culture that we find them creeping into our own conversation. But the rationalization that "everybody does it" and "nobody thinks anything of it" doesn't get us off the hook.

Remember our standard is not what's acceptable to the world, but what's acceptable according to the Word of God. "You are a chosen people, a royal priesthood, a holy nation, a people belonging to God, that you may declare the praises of him who called you out of darkness into his wonderful light" (1 Pet. 2:9). Rude, crude, and crass should never be words that describe us. As Mayor Shinn repeatedly reminded his family in Meredith Willson's *The Music Man*: "Watch your phraseology!"

"Dishonest people conceal their faults from themselves as well as others; honest people know and confess them." —Christian Nestell Bovee

---

Blasphemy. It's so much more than denying the deity of Christ or saying wicked things (as the world so frequently does) about God and his Word. Blasphemy includes being careless, disrespectful, and irreverent in the way we speak of spiritual things and spiritual beings. It's, in our ignorance or arrogance, mocking things we shouldn't mock or making light of things the Bible says should be taken seriously (Jude 7–9). Many of us cringe when other people use the precious name of Jesus as a swear word, but come dangerously close to it ourselves. How often, when we exclaim "Dear Jesus!" or "Oh my God!" are we really pausing for a moment of prayer?

Idle Words. Empty, mindless, meaningless chatter. Talking for the sake of talking, saying things we don't mean, making promises (or threats) we have no intention of following through on. At first glance, they seem harmless. But Scripture warns, "Where words are many, sin is not absent . . ." (Prov. 10:19). The more we talk, talk, talk, the less we listen—to God or others. And the greater the chance that we *will* say something that *is* a sin. The

Bible says, "Avoid godless chatter, because those who indulge in it will become more and more ungodly" (2 Tim. 2:16).

Prideful, Self-Righteous Boasting. Scripture encourages us to "boast in the Lord"—to celebrate all the things he has done in us and through us and publicly give him all the glory and all the honor. What we're *not* to do is boast in our own strength, our own righteousness, and our own accomplishments, drawing attention to ourselves so that we get the credit, the kudos, the respect, or admiration we feel we deserve. (This puffing ourselves up, making ourselves look or sound more important, all too often involves showing others up or putting them down.) The Bible says that God opposes the proud, and that all such boasting and bragging is the province of the wicked. Furthermore, pride goes before a fall (Prov. 16:18). "Let another praise you, and not your own mouth; someone else, and not your own lips" (Prov. 27:2). "Who is wise and understanding among you? Let him show it by his good life, by deeds done in the humility that comes from wisdom" (James 3:13). Our actions sometimes speak much louder than our words.

Nagging, Whining, and Complaining. The book of Proverbs observes that "a quarrelsome wife is like a constant dripping," and that it's "better to live on a corner of the roof" or "in a desert" than in a house with an ill-tempered woman (Prov. 19:13; 21:9, 19). Nagging, whining, grumbling, and complaining— these are symptoms of a selfish, ungrateful heart. A heart that wants its own way in everything—or else! Even God, who has infinite patience, can only take so much of it. The Old Testament tells us that the grumbling of the children of Israel very nearly drove him to distraction—or to destruction, if Moses hadn't intervened—on more than one occasion. Israel's words revealed such a lack of faith and trust in God, his leadership, his guidance, his provision, his power, and his love. It was an insult, an assault on his character (Num. 14:20–34). If we believe that God is in control of our circumstances and that nothing escapes his notice or his care, that whatever comes our way has first come through his hand, then there's no excuse for the attitude that leads to these whiny words. If we recognize that we ourselves are frail, flawed human beings who often sin and frequently fail to live up to others' expectations, then we have no excuse for ripping anyone else "a new one." In fact, we're commanded not to be like ungodly "grumblers and faultfinders" (Jude 16). Instead, Philippians 2:14–15 tells us, "Do everything without complaining or arguing, so that you may become blameless and pure, children of God without fault in a crooked and depraved generation, in which you shine like stars in the universe." We must never forget that our words (a reflection of our hearts) are a witness to our friends and family, our neighbors and coworkers, and the world itself; they are a testimony of who God is and what his people are like.

> "If you don't like something, change it. If you can't change it, change your attitude. Don't complain." —Maya Angelou

Gossip. It's a sin for which women are famous, perhaps because it's an offshoot—a perversion—of a very legitimate contribution we make to our families, neighborhoods, churches, and communities. Women have always built relationships by sharing stories, information, experiences, and ideas. Networking is a part of our nurturing. The trouble is, we don't always know when to hush up! We don't always draw a distinction between what others need to know and what they would enjoy hearing—or what we'd enjoy telling!

"The words of a gossip are like choice morsels; they go down to a man's inmost parts" (Prov. 18:8). From there, they often lead us further into sin. For instance, if we repeat something that isn't true, we're guilty of spreading lies and slander. Freely discussing another's faults and failures often produces in us a sense of superiority and a smug self-righteousness. When we offer our opinion on someone else's attitude or behavior or motives, we're passing judgment on them—something Jesus specifically forbids us to do (Matt. 7:1–5). If what we've heard or said about other people causes us (and others) to reject them, isolate them, persecute them, or otherwise mistreat them, God will hold us responsible for the harm we have done.

> "Alas! they had been friends in youth;
> but whispering tongues can poison
> truth." —Samuel Taylor Coleridge

We've got to learn to stop and ask ourselves: Is what we're about to say true? Is it helpful? Is it necessary—either to have the conversation at all or to include all of the details? Would we be embarrassed if the person we're speaking about somehow overheard what we were saying? Would they?

Before we claim to be speaking in love or out of true concern for someone—"just sharing a prayer request"—we need to remember that "love is patient, love is kind. It does not envy, it does not boast, it is not proud. It is not rude, it is not self-seeking, it is not easily angered, it keeps no record of wrongs. Love does not delight in evil but rejoices with the truth. It always protects, always trusts, always hopes, always perseveres. Love never fails . . ." (1 Cor. 13:4–8). If what we're about to say does not meet this standard, we need to keep it to ourselves.

Backbiting. As a child, I thought "backbiting" meant saying cruel, "biting" things behind someone's back. Much later, I realized I'd been thinking of the definition of "backstabbing." Backbiting is biting someone back—after they've bitten you. It's retaliatory. It's about getting revenge. And it's not acceptable for those of us who love Jesus: "To this you were called, because Christ suffered for you, leaving you an example, that you should follow in his steps. 'He committed no sin, and no deceit was found in his mouth.' When they hurled their insults at him, he did not retaliate; when he suffered, he made no threats. Instead, he entrusted himself to him who judges justly" (1 Pet. 2:21–23).

I think this has to be one of the most difficult things God asks us to do: To trust him to deal with those who falsely accuse us or unfairly attack us, and not allow ourselves to be drawn into a war of words, a bitter and vitriolic "tit for tat." It goes against everything our flesh is made of to turn the other cheek and go on about our Father's business regardless of what's being said behind our backs. It requires enormous discipline and self-control, not to mention grace and faith. There are times when we *must* speak up on behalf of others—to protect the innocent, defend the helpless, and rescue the oppressed (we'll talk more about that in chap. 11). But God is the one in charge of settling scores.

> "The best apology [defense] against false accusers is silence and sufferance, and honest deeds set against dishonest words." —John Milton

"Do not take revenge, my friends, but leave room for God's wrath, for it is written: 'It is mine to avenge; I will repay,' says the Lord" (Rom. 12:19). We can be sure that whether or not we get to see it happen, justice *will* be served. Refusing to retaliate not only protects us from falling into sin ourselves (and thus receiving God's discipline); it serves as a testimony to those around us. And sometimes it leads to reconciliation and restoration, once conviction and repentance have taken place.

In any case—and every case—our goal is always to speak words that live, not words that die. Words that reflect the light of Christ, not words that increase the darkness. As Saint Francis of Assisi prayed:

> Lord, make me an instrument of Your peace.
> Where there is hatred, let me sow love;
> where there is injury, pardon;
> where there is doubt, faith;
> where there is despair, hope;
> where there is darkness, light;
> and where there is sadness, joy.
>
> O Divine Master,
> grant that I may not so much seek to be consoled as to
>   console;
> to be understood as to understand;
> to be loved as to love;
> For it is in giving that we receive,
> it is in pardoning that we are pardoned,
> and it is in dying that we are born to eternal life.
> Amen.

Bible Study

1. Read Psalm 139:1–16 and underline key words or phrases that will help you fully answer the following questions:

    a. What kinds of things does God know about you? (1–4)

    b. How does he know these things? (5–16)

2. Now read Psalm 139:23–24. Make it a prayer from your heart to God. Ask the One who knows you better than you know yourself to help you truthfully answer the following questions:

a. Which "words that die" do you find most likely to cross your lips?

☐ Lies, half-truths, and exaggerations

☐ Profanity and obscenity

☐ Blasphemy

☐ Idle words

☐ Prideful, self-righteous boasting

☐ Nagging, whining, and complaining

☐ Gossip

☐ Backbiting

b. On a scale of 1–10, rate how often these words come out of your mouth:

1   2   3   4   5   6   7   8   9   10

rarely   occasionally   often   habitually   constantly

3. Read Matthew 15:10–11, 15–20.

a. What does not make a person "unclean" or impure (11, 19–20)?

b. What does make a person "unclean" or impure (11, 18–19)?

c. Where does this evil come from (18)?

4. According to Titus 2:11–14, why did Jesus give himself for us?

a. According to 2 Corinthians 7:1, how should we respond? (See also James 4:7–10.)

5. Prayerfully consider some specific things you can do, some concrete steps you can take, to keep your lips free of "words that die." What do you need to change? Who can you enlist for support and accountability? Remember that often the best way to overcome a bad habit is to replace it with a good one.

6. Choose one of the following verses (or one mentioned previously in the chapter) to memorize and meditate on this week.

Psalm 19:14	Ephesians 4:29, 31–32
Proverbs 12:14	Colossians 3:8–10
Proverbs 12:22	1 Peter 3:8–10

7. Take a few moments to record any further thoughts or reflections.

Seven

Words That Sing

"Come, let us sing for joy to the LORD; let us shout aloud to the Rock of our salvation." (Ps. 95:1)

It must have seemed surreal. Beside her stood the baby brother whose diapers she had changed, whose life she had saved all those years ago as she carefully watched him float in a little basket among the bulrushes. Now he was all grown up and a prince, a prophet, a priest, a man of God. Before her surged the waters of the Red Sea, waters that had hours earlier risen up like walls, creating a passageway for the children of Israel to exit Egypt and escape slavery for the freedom of the Promised Land. Moments ago, those same walls had come crashing down on the chariots of the soldiers who pursued them, obliterating the armies of Egypt in one fell swoop.

Looking back, she could see the sovereignty of God—his awesome power and might. Only God could have chosen her brother Moses from birth, saved him from certain death, and sent him to live in the palace where he would learn all the wisdom of Egypt and be trained as a great leader. Only God could have sent him into the desert to complete his education—to humble him and test him and teach him to rely on God alone for his strength. Only God could bring him back stronger than ever, with an unshakeable faith that gave him the courage to confront Pharaoh and demand he set God's people free. Only God could have sent the plagues that put terror in the hearts of the Egyptians so that they not only agreed to set their slaves free, but begged them to leave, showering them with gifts along the way. Only God could have led them to the edge of the Red Sea and then parted the waters—just in time—to reveal his power not only to his own people, but to their enemies as well.

She was overcome with emotion: exhilarated by the victory, humbled by the part God had allowed her and her family to play, and overflowing with awe, with gratitude, with joy. She couldn't help but pour out her heart in worship and call those around her to join in.

"If we could only see the heart of the Father, we would be drawn into praise and thanksgiving more often. It is easy for us to think that God is so majestic and so highly exalted that our adoration makes no difference to him. Our God is not made of stone. His heart is the most sensitive and tender of all. No act goes unnoticed, no matter how insignificant or small. A cup of cold water is enough to put tears in the eyes of God. God celebrates our feeble expressions of gratitude." —Richard J. Foster

"Then Miriam the prophetess . . . took a tambourine in her hand, and all the women went out after her with tambourines and dancing. And Miriam sang to them: 'Sing to the LORD, for he has triumphed gloriously; the horse and his rider he has thrown into the sea'" (Ex. 15:20–21, ESV).

Miriam wasn't the only woman in Scripture to respond to the glory and majesty and mercy of God by bursting into song. Israel's only female Judge, Deborah, bravely led the fearful armies of Israel into battle at God's command. Then she celebrated the victory he gave them with a wildly jubilant song of praise (Judg. 5:1–31). When Elizabeth prophesied over Mary concerning the child that had been conceived in her by the Holy Spirit, the young mother-to-be responded by humbly pouring out her heart to God in a beautiful psalm of praise and thanksgiving—Mary's Song, the Magnificat. "My soul magnifies the Lord, and my spirit rejoices in God my Savior . . . from now on all generations will call me blessed; for he who is mighty has done great things for me, and holy is his name" (Luke 1:46, 48, ESV).

When we see God move in our midst, when we catch just a glimpse of who he is and what he has done for us, it's only natural to respond in awe and gratitude, with words of praise and worship and thanksgiving. And not just in the face of the extraordinary, supernatural, and miraculous, but in the "ordinary" everyday miracles, the beauty and majesty of creation itself. As nineteenth century poet Elizabeth Barrett Browning put it, "Earth's crammed with heaven, and every common bush afire with God. . . ."[1]

Scripture tells us that God created us to glorify him and to enjoy him forever. Nothing brings us more fulfillment than to worship him—to do that which we were created to do. "Worship the LORD in the splendor of his holiness" (Ps. 29:2, NLT).

Over the years, I've wrestled with a lot of spiritual and theological issues, but for some reason, one I've never had trouble with is that God deserves our worship and that it's not arrogant or vain or needy of him to ask for it. He created us so that he could share himself with us—so that we could enjoy all that he is and all that he gives, so that we could revel in his beauty, in his majesty, in his holiness—and respond in heartfelt worship.

If you've ever done something kind or thoughtful or loving or selfless, if you've ever created something beautiful or meaningful, you know how special it is to share it with someone else. In essence, you are giving them the gift of yourself. And if they recognize your thoughtfulness, your effort, and your sacrifice and they have an appreciation for you as the giver—not just the gift—then there's something very special about their expression of thanks. In that moment it blesses you, it blesses them. It brings the two of you closer in new and unexpected ways. And you have just a tiny taste of what the worship of God is all about, why it's so meaningful to him and to us.

In one sense, all of our lives are meant to be worship, everything we are, everything we do, everything we say. But here, I want to focus on what we say—on the way we express our hearts with words that sing: words that express our admiration, our appreciation, our adoration of God. Whether written or spoken or sung, these words, too, have incredible power not only to glorify God and bless his heart, but to bless our hearts. Words that sing inspire us, uplift us, renew us, and refresh us.

"Faith comes from hearing . . ." (Rom. 10:17). As we've already seen, the words we speak, we believe. When our words express our hope in Christ, our faith and trust in him, and when we confess that "God is good, all the time; all the time, God is good"—our hearts and minds receive it and believe it. Whether we express these words in corporate worship, in our personal quiet time, in a small group Bible study, or over coffee at Starbucks with a friend, they have the same effect: they build up our spirits, and through us, the spirits of those around us. It's one reason Ephesians 5:19 urges us to "speak to one another with psalms, hymns, and spiritual songs. Sing and make music in your heart to the Lord."

Praise has a way of putting things into proper perspective, helping us see our circumstances from God's perspective. Our priorities fall into place as we remember why we're here and who we're here for!

Over and over in the Old Testament, God sent his armies into battle with little more than a song of praise on their lips. And that praise was the key to their victory. With a mighty shout, the walls of Jericho fell down (Josh. 6:20). Incredibly, it was often the choir that led the charge. When the people sang God's praises, their enemies fell into confusion and defeated themselves (2 Chron. 20:22).

"Our truest responsibility to the irrationality
of the world is to paint or sing or write,
for only in such response do we find
the truth." —Madeleine L'Engle

By praising God in the midst of his suffering, Job proved that his heart was true—that he loved God and not just his gifts—at the same time giving the devil (who had said otherwise) a black eye (Job 1:1–2:10). A kick in the gut. That's what our praise has the power to do. Considering all the misery the devil has caused, I'm not at all sorry about that. In fact, it gives me great satisfaction. I wish I remembered to praise God more often, just for that very reason.

Seriously. When you think about it, words that sing are some of our most powerful weapons against the enemy of our souls. When David played his psalms, the demon that tormented King Saul fell silent. The anger, fear, confusion, and paranoia with which it had filled his heart dissipated, and the evil spirit left him (1 Sam. 16:14–23). I know when my own spirit is under attack, if I sing songs about the blood of Jesus that was shed for me and the victory that he won on Calvary, if I put praise and worship music on in the house or the car or my iPod, the atmosphere instantly changes. For me, it's a good thing, but for the enemy, it becomes extremely uncomfortable and unpleasant—and he leaves!

Words of hope, words of truth, words of faith. These weapons expose the enemy's lies for what they are—and refute them.

In the classic allegory, *Pilgrim's Progress*, author John Bunyan describes the journey of a man named Christian from sin and bondage in the City of Destruction to eternal peace and joy in the Celestial City. Along the way, Christian faces many trials that test his faith. At one point, he passes through a dark valley inhabited by hideous demonic beings that hover about, just out of sight. They begin to whisper the most awful, blasphemous things in Christian's ear. Stumbling along in the dark, Christian mistakes their voices for his own thoughts. He's overcome with horror and shame and self-reproach. How could he think such things? What a terrible wretch he is! Christian staggers under the guilt and despair.

"It seemed intended by the blessed providence of God that I should be blind all my life, and I thank him for the dispensation. If perfect earthly sight were offered me tomorrow I would not accept it. I might not have sung hymns to the praise of God if I had been distracted by the beautiful and interesting things about me." —Fanny Crosby

Down through the ages, many believers have experienced that very same thing. Satan whispers his blasphemies and introduces evil thoughts, and we're shocked and dismayed. We think *we* came up with these vile expressions. We ask ourselves, "Can I really be a Christian and think such a thing?"

In Bunyan's story, Christian is rescued when a friend comes alongside him and begins quoting the Word of God to him, speaking words of truth and goodness and grace. Words that sing God's praises. The demonic beings are forced to flee, and Christian is set free.

So often we mistake the voice of the enemy for that of our own hearts. We feel guilty and ashamed and question our salvation—when what we need to do is rebuke the devil and watch him flee. We need to stop taking credit for his filth, refuse to listen to his lies, and counter every blasphemous thought with the truths of Scripture, words of worship, and praise.

Listen to the joyous proclamation with which Jesus began his earthly ministry. He quoted these words from Isaiah 61:1–3, declaring that he himself was the fulfillment of them:

> The Spirit of the Sovereign Lord is on me,
>> because the Lord has anointed me
>> to preach good news to the poor.
> He has sent me to bind up the brokenhearted,
>> to proclaim freedom for the captives
>> and release from darkness for the prisoners,
> to proclaim the year of the Lord's favor
>> and the day of vengeance of our God,
> to comfort all who mourn,
>> and provide for those who grieve in Zion—
> to bestow on them a crown of beauty
>> instead of ashes,
> the oil of gladness
>> instead of mourning,
> and a garment of praise
>> instead of a spirit of despair.

See what God has done for us? What he promises to do? No matter how difficult the battle, we are more than conquerors through him who loved us. "Neither death nor life, neither angels nor demons, neither our fears for today nor our worries about tomorrow—not even the powers of hell can separate us from God's love" (Rom. 8:38, NLT). The victory has been won. It's already ours. So we have every reason to rejoice. Every reason to choose to put on a "garment of praise" instead of a spirit of heaviness.

"The most important part of our task will be to tell everyone who will listen that Jesus is the only answer to the problems that are disturbing the hearts of men and nations. We will have the right to speak because we can tell from our experience that His light is more powerful than the deepest darkness. How wonderful that the reality of His presence is greater than the reality of the hell about us." —Betsie ten Boom

That's what Paul and Silas did. Just for faithfully preaching the gospel, these men had been severely beaten and thrown into prison, their feet put in the stocks. I guess it would have been understandable if they'd lain there moaning in pain or crying out to God in anguish and despair. But that wasn't how they chose to respond to their circumstances. The Bible tells us that at midnight, Paul and Silas were rejoicing and praising God, singing hymns from their heart to his. God sent an earthquake to shake the prison walls, break their chains, and set Paul and Silas free. Because of their testimony in the midst of suffering and persecution, the jailor and everyone in his household became followers of Jesus Christ (Acts 16:16–34).

Sometimes the most powerful praise comes from the darkest of times.

Perhaps you've heard the story of the successful lawyer, real estate investor, and businessman who lost nearly everything he owned in the Great Chicago Fire of 1871. A year earlier, his only son had died of scarlet fever at the age of four. The man decided that his family—his wife and four daughters— desperately needed a change of scene, so he arranged to take them on a vacation, an extended trip to Europe. At the last minute he was detained by urgent business, but he sent his wife and daughters on ahead, promising to follow them as soon as he could. However, in a freak accident, only a few days after they set sail, their ship collided with another vessel in the middle of the Atlantic Ocean. Horatio Spafford soon received a two-word telegram from his wife: "Saved alone." All four of their girls had drowned. Spafford took the next available ship to England to be with his devastated wife. He asked the captain to let him know when they passed the spot where his daughters had perished. Standing on the deck, looking out over their watery graves, Spafford had a choice to make. He could rail against the injustice, he could throw a tantrum over the unfairness of all that he had suffered. He could "curse God and die" (Job 2:9). Or he could acknowledge that God was God, even when he didn't understand why God allowed things to happen the way they did. Spafford could affirm his faith in God's goodness, in his love and mercy and grace—and declare his trust in him, regardless of his circumstances. Spafford made his choice. Later, on a scrap of paper, he scribbled the words:

When peace, like a river, attendeth my way,
When sorrows like sea billows roll;
Whatever my lot, Thou hast taught me to say,
It is well, it is well with my soul.

Though Satan should buffet, though trials should come,
Let this blest assurance control,
That Christ hath regarded my helpless estate,
And hath shed his own blood for my soul.

As he had stood there worshiping God on the deck of the ship, Spafford's focus shifted to a reality that transcended the tragedy he had suffered: because of what *Jesus* had suffered, he could be forgiven of his sins—all his weaknesses and failures—and have the hope of heaven, a perfect world in which there is no pain or suffering or loss. A place where he would one day experience a beautiful reunion with his precious children.

> My sin, oh the bliss of this glorious thought!
> My sin, not in part but the whole,
> Is nailed to his cross, and I bear it no more,
> Praise the Lord, praise the Lord, O my soul!
>
> And Lord haste the day, when my faith shall be sight,
> The clouds be rolled back as a scroll;
> The trump shall resound, and the Lord shall descend,
> Even so, it is well with my soul.[2]

Spafford's words have since challenged, comforted, encouraged, and inspired millions of believers to praise God in the midst of their own suffering and heartache—to declare their allegiance to and dependence on him, offering up a "sacrifice of praise" as a precious gift to be laid on the altar of God (Heb. 13:15). They, too, have experienced the powerful truth that God inhabits the praises of his people (see Ps. 22:3). God draws us close to him through our praise and worship, and "the reality of His presence is greater than the reality of the hell around us."[3]

In the presence of Jesus, there is a peace that passes all understanding. There is a joy that no one can take away. There is a love that will not let us go. For hundreds of years, hymns like Spafford's have reminded the body of Christ of this life-changing truth and helped us put it into practice. We've drawn near to God—and he has drawn near to us—as we've sung hymns such as:

"Be Still My Soul"

"Blessed Assurance"

"Have Thine Own Way, Lord"

"He Hideth My Soul"

"His Eye Is on the Sparrow"

"His Name Is Wonderful"

"I Am Thine, O Lord"

"I Need Thee Every Hour"

"I'd Rather Have Jesus"

"Jesus Is the Sweetest Name I Know"

"Jesus Loves Me (This I Know)"

"Jesus, Name Above All Names"

"Jesus Paid It All"

"Just as I Am"

"Lead Me to Calvary"

"Mine Eyes Have Seen the Glory" ("Battle Hymn of the Republic")

"Nearer, My God to Thee"

"Take My Life and Let It Be"

"Thou Didst Leave Thy Throne"

"'Tis So Sweet to Trust in Jesus"

"To God Be the Glory"

"Turn Your Eyes upon Jesus"

"When We All Get to Heaven"

Incidentally, the lyrics—and in some cases the music—for every one of the above hymns (and countless others) were written by women. These women gave voice to the hope of every heart that belongs to Jesus, and they let their words sing.

These were real women—women like you and me. Some were wives and mothers and grandmothers; others were single. Many of them faced enormous difficulty and extraordinary hardship. Some were widowed before their very eyes or lost their parents or siblings or children in tragic circumstances. They suffered financial ruin or lived in chronic pain. At one time or another, every one of them experienced some kind of rejection, betrayal, failure, frustration, or discouragement. But they refused to be defeated. They were determined to "hold fast that which is good" (1 Thess. 5:21). They learned what it means to "give thanks in everything" (1 Thess. 5:18).

As they grew in their relationship with Christ, they found that along with the apostle Paul, they could say: "I consider everything a loss compared to the surpassing greatness of knowing Christ Jesus my Lord, for whose sake I have lost all things. I consider them rubbish, that I may gain Christ and be found in him, not having a righteousness of my own . . . but that which is through faith in Christ—the righteousness that comes from God and is by faith" (Phil. 3:8–9).

None of them were perfect women—and neither are we. But that's what makes their testimony (and ours) all the more amazing. Even miraculous: "We have this treasure in jars of clay to show that this all-surpassing power is from God and not from us. We are hard pressed on every side, but not crushed; perplexed, but not in despair; persecuted, but not abandoned; struck down, but not destroyed" (2 Cor. 4:7–9).

The hymnwriters understood the power of praise to lift our gaze from the trials and tribulations of this life and fix it firmly on the One who promised never to leave us or forsake us. The One who holds the whole world in his hands. The One who holds us in his heart.

Leah learned this, too.

Remember Rachel and Leah—the two sisters who were married to Jacob? Genesis 29:18 tells us that Jacob was very much in love with Rachel and worked for seven long years to earn her hand in marriage—only to be tricked by his uncle into marrying her older sister Leah first. This began one of the most bitter family feuds ever recorded in the Bible, as the two sisters constantly competed with each other for their husband's love and affection. Of course, Leah was the loser right from the start. She was the less attractive of the two, the one her father had feared he wouldn't be able to unload. Jacob had never loved her or wanted her. Her sister Rachel now deeply resented her.

In Genesis 29:31, it says that the Lord saw that Leah was "despised"—some translations say "hated." Hated by her own family for something that wasn't her fault, something she had absolutely no control over. So God had compassion on her. It says he "opened her womb" and gave her children, something that Rachel wouldn't have for a very long time. Leah was thrilled to discover that she was pregnant. She thought that by producing Jacob's first heir, she would earn his love and respect. She named her first son Reuben, saying, "The LORD has seen my misery. Surely my husband will love me now."

But he didn't. Leah gave birth to a second son, Simeon, saying, "Because the LORD heard that I am not loved, he gave me this one, too." But Simeon's birth didn't change Jacob's feelings for Leah. With the birth of her third son, Leah was still desperately trying to win her husband's love. Hoping against hope, she named him Levi, meaning "attached," saying, "Now at last my husband will become attached to me, because I have borne him three sons." Can you hear the desperation?

But once again, her hopes were dashed. With the birth of her fourth son, Leah had a revelation. She had finally come to grips with the reality of the situation: nothing she could do would make Jacob love her. So she stopped trying. She stopped looking to her husband for the affection, the approval, the affirmation that he was either unwilling or unable to give. When Judah was born, Leah said simply, "This time I will praise the LORD . . ." (Gen. 29:35).

As Leah discovered, praise has the power to set us free. Free from the kind of festering pain that poisons us. Free from the hurt of unmet needs, expectations, and longings. Free from the fixation on things we cannot control, cannot change, and that—in the light of eternity—are fleeting and will one day fade away. Free to love God with our whole heart and serve him faithfully regardless of (sometimes in spite of) our circumstances.

We can declare with the psalmist, "I will sing to the LORD all my life; I will sing praise to my God as long as I live" (Ps. 104:33); "I will sing to the LORD, for he has been good to me" (Ps. 13:6).

Bible Study

1. Read the story of Jesus and the "sinful woman" in Luke 7:36–50 and answer the following questions.

a. How did the "sinful woman" express her love and gratitude to Jesus (37–38, 44–46)?

b. Try to put yourself in her shoes: A woman whose sins are public knowledge (the subject of much gossip, criticism, and condemnation), entering the home of a Pharisee uninvited, to do something that could not go unnoticed. How might this have been a difficult or costly sacrifice for her? What did she risk? What did she lose?

c. What made her willing to do this? Why was she so grateful (41–43, 47–48)?

d. How did Jesus respond to her sacrifice?

e. To the woman herself (48, 50)?

f. To those who sat in judgment of her (39–47)?

2. Read Ephesians 5:1–2. What sacrifice did Jesus offer to God? Who did he make this sacrifice for?

3. Read 2 Corinthians 2:14–16. When we become "imitators of God," when we follow in Jesus' footsteps, what "aroma" do we give off?

4. Psalm 141:2 says, "May my prayer be set before you like incense; may the lifting up of my hands be like the evening sacrifice." In light of these verses and what we've discussed in this chapter, how does a "sacrifice of praise" please God? What kind of impact does it have on us? On others?

5. Spend some time reflecting on who God is and what he has done for you, and let it inspire you to offer him a "sacrifice of praise." Write your own personal psalm,

an expression from your heart to his. It could be a call to worship or thanksgiving (see Psalms 100; 150), a celebration of the beauty of God's creation (see Psalm 8), a song of confession and repentance (see Psalm 51), a victory chant (see Psalm 47), or even a recounting of your personal/family history and how God has shown himself mighty during the most significant events—or in the most meaningful aspects—of your life (see Psalm 105).

Note: If the thought of writing your own psalm is intimidating to you, keep it simple—a heartfelt paragraph or two. Otherwise, challenge yourself to be creative in your expression. Write it in verse or set it to music; see if you can sing it to the tune of another praise and worship song. You might even illustrate your psalm or scrapbook it. Put it in a frame on your desk or someplace else where you will see it often and be reminded again and again to let your words sing!

6. Choose one of the following verses (or one mentioned previously in the chapter) to memorize and meditate on this week.

Exodus 15:1–2	Romans 11:33–36
1 Chronicles 16:28–29	Hebrews 13:15
Psalm 40:1–3	Revelation 5:12
Psalm 100	Revelation 7:12
Psalm 103:1–4	

Eight

Words That Cry

"My soul yearns, even faints, for the courts of the Lord; my heart and my flesh cry out for the living God." (Ps. 84:2)

It was a quiet, uneventful evening at the Christian radio station where I was working as an "on-air personality" (a deejay). But my stomach was churning. Earlier I'd heard that one of my dearest friends was facing a terrible crisis that was devastating her emotionally and spiritually, even physically. And I was thousands of miles away. On a different continent, in fact. There was not a thing I could do about it. My heart was aching for her. I wanted so much to be there to wrap my arms around her and reassure her of my love, of God's love. I wanted to rescue her somehow and shield her from the pain. I was so distraught on her behalf. The weight of it felt like an anchor or an anvil hanging around my neck.

The phone rang. It was an elderly woman, a listener, calling with a prayer request. Apparently, she thought that in order to understand the nature of her request, I needed to know her personal testimony, her whole family history, and the complete family history of everyone even remotely connected to it. Bless her heart! She was obviously lonely and needed someone to talk to. Technically it was part of my job description to listen and to be there for her. So I did—I was. Truthfully, it was a little difficult to hear her; the call sounded distant, like it was being made from a tunnel. And she mumbled quite a bit, her words and sentences running together. I couldn't really follow it all. I tried to put in an appropriately sympathetic response here and there ("Oh dear!" "Really?" "My goodness."). But as she rambled on and on, my mind wandered back to my friend and the trial she was facing. I felt so frustrated and helpless. I was powerless to do anything to alleviate even a little of her suffering. I was turning it all over and over in mind and getting more and more worked up about it. Suddenly the woman on the other end of the phone almost shouted into the receiver, *"Prayer changes things, you know!"* She repeated the words, for emphasis: "Prayer changes things." Then she mumbled and murmured a few other things before abruptly hanging up. And I sat there with tears streaming down my face. It was as if the Holy Spirit himself had picked up the phone to remind me that I was *not* powerless to help my friend. There was something very important—vitally important—that I could do for her. I could pray. I could cry out to God on her behalf. Scripture says, "The earnest prayer of a righteous person has great power . . ." (James 5:16, NLT).

With words that cry out to God, we intercede for our friends and family, our community and our country. With these words, we express our hopes and dreams, our fears, our needs. We open our hearts to him.

The Bible tells us to "pray continually" (1 Thess. 5:17). "Do not be anxious about anything, but in everything, by prayer and petition, with thanksgiving, present your requests to God" (Phil. 4:6). "Cast all your anxiety on him because he cares for you" (1 Pet. 5:7). "Devote yourselves to prayer, being watchful and thankful" (Col. 4:2). Like praise, prayer has a way of putting things into perspective, helping us walk before God and others with humility.

> "Oh, what a cause of thankfulness it is that we have a gracious God to go to on all occasions! Use and enjoy this privilege and you can never be miserable. Oh, what an unspeakable privilege is prayer." —Lady Maxwell

C. S. Lewis once said, "I pray because I can't help myself. I pray because I'm helpless. I pray because the need flows out of me all the time—waking and sleeping. It doesn't change God—it changes me."

Lewis is right: prayer doesn't change God, in the sense that it doesn't *make* him do something he doesn't already want or intend to do. However, Scripture indicates that it *moves* him to do it—and that without our prayers, he may not. For reasons we may never fully understand, God chooses to use our prayers—chooses to respond to our prayers—as a means of achieving or accomplishing his purposes. He has given us the privilege and responsibility of partnering with him in his work through the power of prayer. Perhaps it's because the interaction between us and him is one of the ways he draws us closer and brings us into a deeper relationship with him. When we communicate with God (both talking *and* listening), we come to know him better, understand him more clearly, and appreciate him more. We learn to trust him and more fully depend or rely on him.

In *The Magician's Nephew* (the prequel to Lewis's *The Lion, the Witch and the Wardrobe*), the Great Lion Aslan sends Polly and Digory and their flying horse Fledge off on an important quest. But when night falls and they still haven't reached their destination, the children grow hungry, and realize they have nothing to eat.

> Polly and Digory stared at one another in dismay.
> "Well, I *do* think someone might have arranged about our meals," said Digory.
> "I'm sure Aslan would have, if you'd asked him," said Fledge.
> "Wouldn't he know without being asked?" said Polly.
> "I've no doubt he would," said the Horse, (still with his mouth full [of grass]). "But I've a sort of idea he likes to be asked."[1]

In Matthew 6:8, Jesus assured his disciples, "Your Father knows what you need before you ask him." But then he went on to give them instructions on how to pray. In Matthew 7:7, he said, "Ask and it will be given to you; seek and you will find; knock and the door will be opened to you." James 4:2 explains, "You do not have, because you do not ask God." The message is clear: Our loving heavenly Father knows everything his children need, and he longs to give it to us—he just wants us to ask!

> "Any concern too small to be turned into a prayer is too small to be made into a burden." —Corrie ten Boom

The Bible tells us that Hannah was a woman who knew how to ask. She knew where to take her hurt and heartache. Hannah was barren, at a time when a woman's worth was measured by the number of children she produced. To be childless was considered a shame and embarrassment, even a sign of God's disapproval. To make matters worse, Hannah's husband had another wife who had already given him many sons and daughters.

Hannah's husband was an exceptional man. He loved Hannah deeply, regardless of whether she produced any heirs. In fact, he went out of his way to give her preferential treatment in the family circle. He tried to be as encouraging and supportive as he knew how. But Hannah's need was too great; she could not be comforted by her husband's love. His other wife constantly gloated over her and tormented her. "This went on year after year. Whenever Hannah went up to the house of the LORD, her rival provoked her till she wept and would not eat" (1 Sam. 1:7).

Isn't that just like the enemy of our souls? At a time when we should be joyously anticipating an encounter with God, at a time when we have the opportunity to draw strength and comfort from his presence, Satan stirs up our deepest heartaches and fills our minds with painful memories or fresh new hurts. But Hannah refused to be deterred. In the tabernacle, she wept and prayed and poured out her heart to God. She promised that if he gave her a son, she would give the boy back to him. If only he would hear her cry.

"In my distress I called to the LORD; I cried to my God for help. From his temple he heard my voice . . ." (Ps. 18:6).

God did hear the cry of Hannah's heart, and he answered her prayer. He gave her the desire of her heart. Not long after she'd been so wracked with grief, her body shaking with pain as she prayed (to the point where the priest mistook her for a drunk!), Hannah returned to the house of the Lord triumphant. She brought her son, Samuel, to be dedicated to the service of God. She burst into a psalm of praise, a prayer of thanksgiving: "My heart rejoices in the LORD! The LORD has made me strong. Now I have an answer for my enemies; I rejoice because you rescued me. No one is holy like the LORD! There is no one besides you; there is no Rock like our God" (1 Sam. 2:1–2, NLT). Her joy only grew with the births of her other three sons and two daughters. Because she had brought her need to God, because she had asked, he had given her *more* than she could ask or even imagine (Phil. 4:5–7; Eph. 3:20).

We can ask God out loud or in our hearts or on the pages of a journal. We can pray privately or corporately, at church or in the car or over the kitchen sink. We can pray with a friend over the phone or in an e-mail. Sometimes it helps to have a system, a method for lifting up all the prayer needs that come to our attention. It helps to have a way to remember who or what we've prayed for and when, so that we can give thanks and celebrate when those prayers are answered. We can pray the prayers we find in the Scriptures. We can repeat the words of a profound and carefully thought-out prayer that someone else has written. Or we can talk to God as casually and naturally as we would our best friend. Some women I know like to use an acronym like A.C.T.S. (Adoration, Confession, Thanksgiving, Supplication) to keep in mind that there's more to prayer than running down a list of requests or complaints.

The most important thing is that no matter when or where or how we cry out to God in prayer, we have the assurance that he hears us and that our prayers will always be answered (Ps. 34:17; 145:19).

Sometimes the answer is an immediate and resounding "yes!" A miracle takes place before our very eyes. The laws of nature are temporarily suspended by their Creator. The heavens open, the waters part, the way is made clear. A hard heart is inexplicably softened. A closed mind is suddenly opened. Looking back, we discover a pattern, a plan, a purpose in what seemed like the most random of circumstances, the most inconsequential actions or choices, the most insignificant details. We can see the hand of God so clearly. The pages of this book could be filled with stories of answers to prayer—yours, mine, people in Scripture, people in history, and people we know. It's good to tell these stories over and over again, to remind ourselves of how God has intervened in the past so that we're encouraged to trust him with the future. It's also good to remember that the answers to our prayers may bring us more than we bargained for. They may require more from us than we thought. "God answers sharp and sudden on some prayers, and thrusts the thing we have prayed for in our face, a gauntlet with a gift in it."[2] Getting what we asked for can force us to make greater sacrifices or meet greater challenges than we could have anticipated. If you've ever prayed for patience, you know what I mean!

> "You need not cry very loud; He is nearer to us than we think." —Brother Lawrence

Sometimes the answer is not so immediate or so readily apparent. God says, "Yes, but not now." Or "wait." Though it seems to us that he's not listening—that he's too busy or that he has forgotten us—he is actually hard at work bringing all the pieces of the puzzle together, orchestrating the necessary circumstances and preparing our hearts and the hearts of those around us. Often there's far more at stake than we realize and so many different factors we haven't even considered.

The book of Daniel gives us an amazing behind-the-scenes look at another reason the answers sometimes take so long to come our way. The prophet Daniel had been fasting and praying for three weeks, urgently seeking a Word from the Lord. It was one of those critical situations where time is of the essence. He desperately needed wisdom and guidance, but none came.

Then suddenly an angel appeared, saying: "Do not be afraid, Daniel. Since the first day that you set your mind to gain understanding and to humble yourself before your God, your words were heard, and I have come in response to them" (Dan. 10:12). From the first day? Then what was the hold up? The angel explained: "For twenty-one days the spirit prince of the kingdom of Persia blocked my way. Then Michael, one of the archangels, came to help me . . ." (v. 13, NLT). There had been an epic battle between the angelic messengers of God and the demonic beings who had authority over the region. But at last the messenger was free, and Daniel would finally receive the answer he had been waiting for (see Dan. 10:1–20).

"Certain thoughts are prayers. There are moments when, whatever be the attitude of the body, the soul is on its knees." —Victor Hugo

---

Ephesians 6:12–13 tells us that there are spiritual forces at work in the heavenly realms, unseen battles going on all around us. We can't be faint-hearted or easily discouraged when we don't see instant results. We may be right on the verge of a breakthrough, if we only press in and persevere in prayer. It could be that the answer is already on the way.

Of course, sometimes the answer is "no." Matthew 7:11 assures us that our Father in heaven knows how to give good gifts to those who ask him. But he doesn't always give us what we ask *for*. Because he is all-wise and all-knowing (not just all-powerful) and because he is good and kind, and because he loves us, he sometimes overrules our requests. He may give us what we need rather than what we want. Or what we really and truly want, but don't know to ask for. God knows not only the plan and purpose he has for us, but for our family, our community, our nation, the whole world. And he knows how one thing affects another and another. Only he can see all of the bigger picture. Lest we forget, his goal is not just to make us comfortable or happy for a moment, but to make us more like Jesus—which will bring us joy for all eternity.

It's not necessarily that our requests are bad or wrong. Sometimes they're good. King David wanted to express his love and gratitude to God by building him a magnificent temple—to bring glory and honor to his name. What was wrong with that? Nothing. But God said no. With great tenderness and affection,

God explained that it was good that it was in David's heart to do it. It blessed God that David wanted to honor him that way. But that wasn't a part of God's plan for the king. It was a job that he had assigned to someone else—David's son, Solomon (2 Sam. 7:1–29).

> "God's gifts put man's best dreams to shame." —Elizabeth Barrett Browning

I once heard this truth so beautifully expressed in the words of a song by Suzanne Gaither Jennings and Bonnie Keen: "When God says 'no,' He's always saying 'yes': 'Yes, I will protect you. Yes, my child, I know what's best. Yes to better dreams you have yet to know.' There's a hidden affirmation when God says 'no.'"[3]

Sometimes it feels like God has said no—or at least "not yet"—to so many of my most precious dreams, my most earnest and heartfelt requests. (Though when I'm not feeling sorry for myself, I have to admit there are so many to which he's said yes!) But I keep crying out to him, because I know he hears me. I know he understands the pain I'm going through. When I'm speaking to him, he often speaks to me. Interrupts me, even. Comforts me and strengthens me and reminds me of all the many reasons I can trust him and his love for me. He reminds me that he's doing something so much bigger than what I can see.

As a Civil War soldier once observed:

I asked God for strength, that I might achieve,
   I was made weak, that I might learn humbly to obey.
I asked for health, that I might do greater things,
   I was given infirmity, that I might do better things.
I asked for riches, that I might be happy,
   I was given poverty, that I might be wise.

I asked for power, that I might have the praise of men,
  I was given weakness, that I might feel the need of God.
I asked for all things, that I might enjoy life,
  I was given life, that I might enjoy all things.
I got nothing that I asked for—but everything I had hoped
    for.
  Almost despite myself, my unspoken prayers were
    answered.
I am, among all men, most richly blessed.

God always answers our prayers. Sometimes he says yes. Sometimes he says wait. Sometimes he says no. The key is to keep the lines of communication open. Keep coming to him, calling on him, and crying out to him. The more time we spend in his presence, the more we experience his power at work in us and through us.

Bible Study

1. How would you describe your "prayer life"?

   ☐ Great! It's such a vital discipline, an integral part of my relationship with Christ.

   ☐ Pretty good. I pray fairly often; I even keep a prayer journal or follow a certain schedule.

   ☐ Okay, I guess. Sometimes it's hit or miss.

   ☐ Not so great. Actually I feel pretty guilty about not praying more.

   ☐ Prayer life? What prayer life?

2. What would you say are the greatest obstacles or challenges you face in maintaining a regular, disciplined prayer life?

☐ Time—not enough hours in the day.

☐ Focus—my mind wanders a lot.

☐ Faith—I have trouble believing that God will answer or that he can or will do as I ask.

☐ Coherence—I struggle to find the right words to say.

☐ Lack of knowledge or instruction—I feel like I'm not doing it right.

☐ Disorganization—I don't know where to start or how to keep all the different prayer needs/ requests straight.

Spend some time brainstorming ways you can overcome these obstacles. (For instance, could you go over your prayer list when you're on the treadmill instead of watching TV? Could you create a notebook with pictures of loved ones to look at as you lift them up in prayer?) Ask Christian friends and mentors what works for them. Or check out some of the recommended resources at the back of this book.

4. Read Mark 9:17–27. What problem or obstacle did the father in this story face? What prevented his request from being granted?

   a. What did Jesus tell him?

   b. How did the father respond?

   c. Ultimately, how did God answer the father's request? Did he say yes or no?

5. Read Hebrews 5:7–9. According to Hebrews 5:7, why were Jesus' prayers heard?

    a.   What phrase in his prayers indicates this condition of his heart (see Matt. 26:36–46, esp. 39, 42)?

    b.   Did God say yes to his Son's request?

    c.   What did Jesus learn from the answer (Heb. 5:8)?

    d.   What greater purpose did this serve (Heb. 5:9)?

    e.   What similar lesson did the apostle Paul learn, according to 2 Corinthians 12:7–9?

6. Choose one of the following verses (or one mentioned previously in the chapter) to memorize and meditate on this week.

Psalm 23	Philippians 4:6–7
Matthew 6:9–13	Colossians 4:2
Matthew 18:20	James 5:13–16
John 14:13–14	1 Peter 5:6–7
Ephesians 6:16–18	

7. Take a few moments to record any further thoughts or reflections.

Nine

Words That Reach

"You will be my witnesses, telling people about me everywhere—in Jerusalem, throughout Judea, in Samaria, and to the ends of the earth." (Acts 1:8, NLT)

The very first witnesses to the resurrected Christ were women. After his death and resurrection, at a time and in a culture in which a woman's word (a woman's testimony) counted for nothing in a court of law, Jesus chose to appear to women first. Perhaps it was because the women were the ones who had stayed with him to the bitter end. While his other disciples went into hiding, in fear of their lives, the women stood sobbing at the foot of the cross. As gruesome and agonizing and horrifying as it was, they never left his side.

Then again, perhaps he appeared to them first because traditionally it belonged to women to welcome the king returning from battle triumphant and to proclaim his victory over the enemy, to celebrate it with singing and dancing in the streets.

"The Lord gives the word; the women who announce the news are a great host" (Ps. 68:11, ESV).

Of course, these witnesses didn't realize at first what they were there to do. The women went to the garden weeping. They thought the King had fallen in the battle, and they wanted to honor him with a proper burial. But the tomb was empty. It looked as though the grave had been robbed, desecrated. Mary Magdalene sobbed, "They have taken my Lord away . . . and I don't know where they have put him" (John 20:13). The man she mistook for a gardener asked her a question:

"Woman," he said, "why are you crying? Who is it you are looking for?"

She answered, "Sir, if you have carried him away, tell me where you have put him, and I will get him."

Jesus said to her, "Mary."

She knew that voice. He had called her name before. Mary sprang toward him and cried out, "Rabboni!"—"Teacher!" (see John 20:10–18; Luke 24:1–10).

She would have fallen at his feet and stayed there for hours, weeping tears of joy. But Jesus had something he wanted her to do. A precious task, an important assignment: she was to go immediately and tell the rest of the disciples the good news: "He has risen, just as he said!" (Matt. 28:6).

Women were the first human beings to proclaim Jesus' victory over sin, death, and the grave. And it is still our privilege, our responsibility—along with our brothers—to proclaim it. "You are a chosen people, a royal priesthood, a holy nation, a people belonging to God, that you may declare the praises of him who called you out of darkness into his wonderful light" (1 Pet. 2:9). "For God, who said, 'Let light shine out of darkness,' made his light shine in our hearts to give us the light of the knowledge of the glory of God in the face of Christ" (2 Cor. 4:6).

There is so much darkness in the world around us. So many lost and lonely. So many hopeless, hurting people. People who live desperate and defeated lives, even though the victory has been won.

"How can they call on him to save them unless they believe in him? And how can they believe in him if they have never heard about him? And how can they hear about him unless someone tells them?" (Rom. 10:14, NLT).

> "There are two ways of spreading
> light: to be the candle or the mirror
> that reflects it." —Edith Wharton

How can *we* be silent? How can we fail to reach the lost with the good news? Jesus is Victor. He has overcome. "Thanks be to God, who always leads us in triumphal procession in Christ and through us spreads everywhere the fragrance of the knowledge of him" (2 Cor. 2:14).

Scripture teaches that some of us have been given a special gift or talent—as well as a passion—for evangelism, for leading others to faith in Christ (Eph. 4:11). The fact that it comes easily, almost naturally (or rather, supernaturally) doesn't mean we're not responsible to do all that we can to develop and strengthen our gifts, sharpen our skills, and heighten our sensitivity to the leading of the Holy Spirit. It also doesn't get those of us who have other gifts off the hook: "Therefore go and make disciples of all nations, baptizing them in the name of the Father and of the Son and of the Holy Spirit, and teaching them to obey everything I have commanded you . . ." (Matt. 28:19–20).

Being a witness is something that every believer is called to, whether it's also our "spiritual gift" or not. But it doesn't have to be as intimidating as it sometimes sounds. Put simply, a "witness" is someone who shares what she has seen and heard. And that's what Jesus has asked us to do: to be his witnesses. We are to tell others what we have heard him say, what we have seen him do, and what we have come to know about his character. What we have experienced by being in a relationship with him.

So every one of us has a story, a testimony, a witness, whether we realize it or not! Not because we have all the answers or we've got it all together. We're still learning and growing in God's grace. Our stories are powerful, because they are so real. They resonate with those who hear them. People can relate! They want to know more about the Man we've fallen in love with, the One whose love has changed us forever. They want to experience this kind of love for themselves.

This is why the devil tries so hard to silence these stories. To silence us.

Sometimes those who've had a more "colorful" past find themselves wrestling with guilt, shame, and regret. They know that God has forgiven them, redeemed them, transformed them. But as they glance at the perfect-looking people sitting in the pew next to them, they hear the devil whisper: "If they knew about your past, they wouldn't be so friendly. If they knew what kind of a person you used to be, you wouldn't be welcome here. They'd never let you be a part of this ministry or that outreach." When you feel like a second-class citizen, you tend to keep your head down and your mouth shut.

"I am only one, but still I am one. I cannot do everything, but still I can do something; and because I cannot do everything, I will not refuse to do something that I can do." —Helen Keller

Funnily enough, those of us who've grown up in the church often feel the same way—like second-class citizens. We wish our stories were as spectacular as the testimonies of others we hear.

The devil tells us we have no story. "What's exciting or miraculous about a five-year-old praying the sinner's prayer?" Like the older brother in Jesus' parable, we watch everyone make a fuss over the prodigal, feeling ignored and left out ourselves. We wrestle with guilt over our sin just as deeply—maybe more—because we can't excuse it or explain it by saying, "That was before I knew Jesus." Or, "Back then, I didn't know any better." We've always known better, which to us makes it all the more shameful. So though we know that we, too, have been forgiven, redeemed, and transformed, we, too, keep quiet.

But what does Scripture teach us about all of this?

Well, there are many dramatic stories in the Bible of people who came to faith later in life—former thieves, prostitutes, murderers, adulterers, drunkards, the demon-possessed, even crooked politicians and corrupt religious leaders. And of course there are your "garden-variety" sinners—ordinary people who simply lived the kind of life a person lives when they have no particular moral code, when they don't have a faith that gives them guidelines to follow. Their stories are wonderful examples of the power of God to turn someone's world upside down—to change their hearts and lives miraculously and completely. It's something he still does today.

Others have a different kind of testimony, a different story. Timothy had known the Scriptures "from infancy" (2 Tim. 3:15). Of course he wasn't perfect; no one is. He needed a Savior like everyone else. But he learned this truth at a very early age. He grew up in a household of faith surrounded by godly influences. As a young man, he went right into a life of ministry and Christian service. Timothy's story is a wonderful example of the power of God at work in a different way—the power to get hold of a child's heart at a young age and to keep that child from ever wandering too far from the faith in the first place. It's something he still does today.

Some people need to hear that God can lift you out of the gutter; others need to know he can keep you from falling into it. Either way, it takes a miracle—it requires a power greater than our own, a power we do not possess. So whatever our background, whatever our story, it's God who gets the glory.

"If I could give you information of my life it would be to show how a woman of very ordinary ability has been led by God in strange and unaccustomed paths to do in His service what He has done in her. And if I could tell you all, you would see how God has done all, and I nothing. I have worked hard, very hard, that is all; and I have never refused God anything." —Florence Nightingale

There are women who are called to be full-time missionaries, to devote their lives to preaching the gospel to foreign people groups in faraway places. Some of them will live (or have lived) through dramatic experiences that suddenly give them a spotlight, a specific opportunity to stand up and say something to people who are eager to hear.

Others can only dream of such things. I've known more than one precious woman so full of gratitude for all that God had done for her—she wished she could do great things for him. She wanted to shout it from the mountaintops and tell the whole wide world about his amazing love. She felt sure she'd be willing to make any sacrifice to demonstrate her love for him. If only he would ask her. . . .

The gospel of Mark tells us about a young man who felt this way. He had been possessed by a legion of evil spirits. "Night and day among the tombs and in the hills he would cry out and cut himself with stones" (Mark 5:5). Then Jesus came and set him free. In an instant the demons were gone. The man was no longer tortured by their presence. The townspeople were amazed when they saw the young man clothed and in his right mind, sitting at Jesus' feet. No, more than amazed—they were terrified. They asked Jesus to go away and leave them alone.

As Jesus got into the boat, the young man begged to be allowed to go with him. He was eager to leave everything behind and follow Jesus (something some of the other disciples had been reluctant to do). But Jesus said no. He wouldn't let him. Instead, Jesus gave him a different assignment: "Go home to your family and tell them how much the Lord has done for you . . ." (Mark 5:19).

See, some of us are called to the mission field overseas, and some of us are called to the mission field in our own family. After all, they're the ones who know us best; they're the ones who see the greatest change in our lives. And their salvation is no less important to Jesus than the millions we will never meet. Though it may have seemed like a small thing, Scripture tells us the young man did just as Jesus asked.

Are we willing to do the same?

"Be brave and dare with a holy
boldness." —Teresa of Avila

Naomi was. Her faith had such an impact on her daughter-in-law, Ruth, that the younger woman was willing to give up everything she loved, leave behind everything she knew: "Where you go I will go, and where you stay I will stay. Your people will be my people and your God my God" (Ruth 1:16).

Today we call it "friendship evangelism"—living our lives in such a way that others are drawn to the hope that lies within us. "In your hearts set apart Christ as Lord. Always be prepared to give an answer to everyone who asks you to give the reason for the hope that you have . . ." (1 Pet. 3:15).

Jesus said to shout it from the housetops—though he didn't mean that we should make a scene (Matt. 10:27). In those days, roofs were flat and functioned as our patios and porches do today. Anything interesting or newsworthy traveled from house to house as neighbors called out to each other across the way. We're more likely to relay information over coffee or scrapbooking, sitting on the sidelines at sports practice or dance class, or chatting in a doctor's office, at the post office, or in the bank. We post all the latest on our social networking sites, message boards, and blogs. Think how readily we share where we got such a deal on the shoes we're wearing or which stores are having a "can't miss" sale. Just as readily and as naturally—and with that same breathless enthusiasm—why not share what God's been doing in our hearts and lives today?

I love the psalmist's declaration:

As for me, I will always have hope;
    I will praise you more and more.
My mouth will tell of your righteousness,
    of your salvation all day long,
    though I know not its measure.
I will come and proclaim your mighty acts, O Sovereign
    LORD;
    I will proclaim your righteousness, yours alone.
Since my youth, O God, you have taught me,
    and to this day I declare your marvelous deeds.
Even when I am old and gray,
    do not forsake me, O God,
till I declare your power to the next generation,
    your might to all who are to come. (Ps. 71:14–18)

Sometimes it takes a little practice, a little preparation, a little thought about what God's given us to say, as well as when and where and how—and to whom—he might want us to say it. It's not a bad idea to memorize a few key Scriptures, read a book, or take a class on personal evangelism when it's offered at your local church.[1]

But remember it's not how learned or articulate or persuasive we are. "Where is the wise man? Where is the scholar? Where is the philosopher of this age? Has not God made foolish the wisdom of the world? . . . Brothers, think of what you were when you were called. Not many of you were wise by human standards; not many were influential; not many were of noble birth. But God chose the foolish things of the world to shame the wise; God chose the weak things of the world to shame the strong" (1 Cor. 1:20, 26–27).

It's the Holy Spirit who brings the conviction that leads to repentance. It's Jesus who saves. What we can do is pray for wisdom and guidance, sensitivity, courage, boldness. We can be willing to be his voice and trust him to give us the words to say. Let him speak through us to reach someone else today.

Bible Study

1. After Jesus ascended into heaven and the Holy Spirit descended on the disciples, Peter preached a sermon at which three thousand men and women became true believers (Acts 2:14–41). "And more were added to their number daily."

   a. Read Acts 4:13. What surprised the Sanhedrin—the Jewish religious leaders—about Peter and John?

   b. To what did they attribute this?

2. What had Jesus promised his disciples in Matthew 10:18–20?

3. First Peter 3:14–15, tells us not to be fearful or afraid to share the reason for the hope that we have, but

to remember who we are (or *whose* we are) and to be prepared, ready to give an answer to anyone who asks us. This exercise is meant to help you prepare to share your story, your testimony with others. Take some time this week to make a list of the most spiritually significant experiences of your life—the key moments, the turning points, the things that have shaped you and made you who you are today. Here are some questions to get you started:

a. How did you come to faith in Christ? Were you raised in a Christian home or did you discover Jesus later in life? Was it a specific moment in time or a gradual process? What made you want to give your heart to him?

b. What are the greatest challenges you've faced, the most difficult things to overcome? Have you had physical issues (health problems)? Family issues? Financial struggles? Emotional or spiritual battles? What hurts and disappointments have you wrestled with? What have been the low points?

c. What about the high points? What are the greatest miracles or answers to prayer that you've received? How have you experienced God's presence in the midst of your "trials and tribulations"—or in the peaceful, ordinary, everyday moments of life?

d. What have you learned about yourself through all of this? What have you learned about God? How might these insights be beneficial to someone else going through a similar experience?

e. Do you have a "life verse," a favorite Scripture (or Scriptures) that—looking back over your life so far—could be your theme, your motto, or your mission statement?

If you've never considered these questions before, you may want to take some time over the next few weeks or even months to dig deep and discover what your story is all about. Keep a record of your insights and observations about your spiritual journey—not only for yourself, but for your loved ones. Write it in a journal or scrapbook it. Talk about it with trusted friends—hear how it sounds when you say it out loud. See what questions they have that might lead you to further insights. If you're ready to share with a broader audience, volunteer to give your testimony at church, in a Sunday school class, or in a small group Bible study. Post it on your Web page, message board, or blog.

4. Ask the Holy Spirit to show you specific people or groups of people that he has given you the opportunity to be a witness to. Prayerfully consider how he might want you to reach out to them.

5. Choose one of the following verses (or one mentioned previously in the chapter) to memorize and meditate on this week.

Isaiah 52:7   2 Corinthians 4:6

Matthew 5:14–16   1 Peter 2:9

Matthew 28:18–20   1 Peter 3:15

6. Take a few moments to record any further thoughts or reflections—or a prayer.

Ten

Words That Teach

"Men are what their mothers made them." —Ralph Waldo Emerson

She had not only brought him into the world and given him life, she had given *her* life to raise him to be a strong, courageous, intelligent, responsible, hard-working, God-fearing man. It took a lot of blood, sweat, and tears to see him through a stormy adolescence and into mature adulthood. But a woman's work is never done, and this woman—the queen—could not rest until she had taught her son the one thing that would have the greatest impact on his future: how to choose a wife. This one decision, how to find a good woman with whom to share his life, would impact every other decision he made for the rest of his life.

The queen knew that, like most young men, her son would quite naturally be drawn to a woman with outward (physical) beauty and that he would—as men have done the world over—equate that outer beauty with inner virtue. He would assume that a woman who is beautiful on the outside is beautiful on the inside. It could be a costly, even tragic mistake. One that would bring him heartache after heartache. The prince's mother had to warn him that "pretty is as pretty does." She had to tell him that in reality, "Charm is deceptive, and beauty is fleeting; but a woman who fears the LORD is to be praised" (Prov. 31:30).

The queen explained to her son that having a godly woman for a wife is a man's greatest treasure. And since outward beauty is *not* a reliable indicator, she listed the kind of things he should look for. First and foremost, he should choose a woman who loves God and follows after him wholeheartedly. A woman who is generous, thoughtful, diligent, disciplined, and industrious. A woman who is responsible with her resources. A woman who cares for the needs of her family and her community. And, since women have a way with words—since her future husband and children would be heavily influenced and guided by her counsel—it was important that she have this key attribute: "She speaks with wisdom, and faithful instruction is on her tongue" (Prov. 31:26). Or as the Amplified Version puts it, "She opens her mouth in skillful and godly Wisdom, and on her tongue is the law of kindness [giving counsel and instruction]."

For once, the young prince was listening. He took his mother's advice. He found it valuable enough that when he became king, he recorded her words of wisdom for future generations, which is how this oracle (inspired message or prophetic word) that "his mother taught him" came to be included in the sayings of King Lemuel in the book of Proverbs (Prov. 31:1). It was a woman herself—the Queen Mother—who painted for us the picture of true feminine beauty and virtue we now refer to as "the Proverbs 31 Woman."

As women, it is a part of our God-given privilege and responsibility to teach and train and mentor the next generation, to pass on what we have learned for the benefit of others. We're called to be godly role models, to speak God's truth into every life we touch. It's our nature to nurture, which, according to the dictionary, means "to nourish, to feed; to educate; train; to help grow or develop; to cultivate; to encourage."

Whether we have children of our own or not, whether our children are grown or not, there are people in all of our lives whom we "mother." Nieces and nephews, godchildren and grandchildren. The younger brothers and sisters with whom we once shared a home. The younger brothers and sisters with whom we share a faith—members of the body of Christ. Younger neighbors, teammates, coworkers, and friends.

For thousands of years, women have been sharing what they know with other women. We have been giving each other advice, instruction, and encouragement and teaching each other the information or skills we've acquired. These days we do it most often over coffee, in our book clubs, at our moms' groups, at our Bible studies, or on message boards and social networking sites rather than at the barn-raisings and quilting bees that brought our great-grandmothers together. (I'm convinced that "nurturing nature" is a big part of the appeal of all the cooking, decorating, and home living shows that dominate cable television.)

"I touch the future. I teach."
—Christa McAuliffe

Some of us have a spiritual gift or specific talent for teaching. Being a teacher is who we are, not just something we do. For some of us, "teacher" is our official title—our job description. We've found our calling in the classroom or in some type of formal educational setting. But all of us, by virtue of our womanhood, are born teachers. We teach our families, we teach our friends. We teach our coworkers, our communities, and our churches. We teach life skills, relationship skills, and career skills. We teach factual information. We teach our observations, our opinions, our values, and our priorities. We teach our principles, convictions, and beliefs. We teach the Scriptures.

Over the years there has been some controversy concerning the role of women in the church—whether or not women should be pastors or Bible teachers. That's obviously not the focus of this book, but it does bear mentioning here.

> "My mother taught me by her example that Jesus is everything. He was the wellspring of her love and joy and peace that overflowed into our home. . . . I have no doubt that the reason I love Jesus and I love my Bible is because she did, and she planted those seeds in my heart long ago." —Anne Graham Lotz

In both the Old Testament and the New Testament, women were prophets and judges and queens. We've seen that during his earthly ministry, Jesus unfailingly treated women with compassion, kindness, and respect. They were among his most faithful disciples. Women were clearly involved in leadership of the early church. They are featured prominently in the book of Acts and mentioned repeatedly in most of the letters written by the apostle Paul and the other disciples. (Many of these letters are actually addressed to or include special greetings to specific women.)

Yet when the apostle Paul gives instructions for pastors, he assumes they will be men. There are passages of Scripture that specify that men (and not women) are to hold specific offices or leadership positions in the church. Throughout the Scriptures, we learn that God has given men and women different roles in the family, in society, and in the body of Christ (see for instance,

Eph. 5:21–33). The buck has to stop somewhere, and the Bible says it stops with the man—the husband or father or pastor—that God has put in charge of a given family or church.

In his instructions on worship, Paul writes, "A woman should learn in quietness and full submission. I do not permit a woman to teach or to have authority over a man; she must be silent" (1 Tim. 2:11–12). Yet as Paul himself pointed out, both men and women are created in the image of God and have equal standing before him (Gal. 3:26–29). Like men, women are recipients of the gifts of the Holy Spirit, which include preaching and teaching gifts (Acts 2:1–4; 1 Cor. 12:7–11, 27–31). "I will pour out my Spirit on all people. Your sons and daughters will prophesy. . . . Even on my servants, both men and women, I will pour out my Spirit in those days" (Joel 2:28–29). Women are not excluded or excused from the responsibility to contribute to the building up of the body of Christ.

So what could Paul have meant when he called for women to be "silent" in church? A number of reputable Bible scholars have suggested that at a time and in a culture where women's rights were severely restricted, some women in the church were having trouble adjusting to their newfound freedom in Christ. Unlike their fathers and brothers and husbands, most of them would not have been taught the Scriptures from childhood—little girls didn't go to Hebrew school. But now they were eager to make their voices heard, even when they didn't know what they were talking about! Far from being helpful, their contribution to the worship service often ended up being disruptive and distracting. This is why Paul told Timothy that he should put a stop to it.

That kind of scenario reminds me of late-night comedy sketches featuring a character called Emily Litella, played years ago by comedian Gilda Radner. Poor Emily was always getting a bee in her bonnet. She'd appear on the local news channel with a blistering commentary expressing outrage about some disturbing social injustice. The trouble was, she never got her facts straight. She misunderstood the issues at hand. She'd exclaim, "What's this I hear about a Supreme Court decision on a deaf penalty? That's terrible! Deaf people have enough problems as it is!" She'd rant and rave for two or three minutes, before someone could inform her that the Court had made a decision regarding the *death* penalty. Stopped dead in her tracks, she'd drop her head and sheepishly apologize: "Oh. Never mind." One of the reasons Radner's sketches were so hilarious is because they hit so close to home. Let's be honest. We all know women who go off half-cocked, just like Emily; maybe we've done it once or twice ourselves!

At times we all need to be humble and quiet and respectful of others while we grow in our understanding and learn all that we can. We need to be diligent to study the Scriptures carefully and thoroughly, so that we know what we're talking about. "Let the word of Christ dwell in you richly as you teach and admonish one another with all wisdom . . ." (Col. 3:16).

We also need to do a heart check and make sure that we're not "usurping authority" (1 Tim. 2:12, KJV), grasping for power or position, and that our desire to teach is not motivated by a longing for significance, special recognition, attention, approval, or applause. James warned, "Not many of you should presume to be teachers . . . because you know that we who teach will be judged more strictly" (James 3:1). We will be held accountable, if, God forbid, we lead others astray. How many of us could say without reservation, "Follow my example, as I follow the example of Christ" (1 Cor. 11:1)?

Today, even churches that take a very conservative position on women in leadership usually have female Sunday school teachers, nursery and children's church and youth workers, women teaching other women in small group Bible studies, etc. Others have female women's ministry directors or pastors of women's ministry. Some have women in leadership roles with leadership titles that they share with their husbands. And still others make no distinction at all between men and women in the service of the church.

Regardless of what position our local church takes, whether it's in an official capacity or not, the fact is that we *do* teach others. And unquestionably, Christian women are called, even commanded, to teach and train and mentor other women: "The older women . . . are to give good counsel and be teachers of what is right and noble . . ." (Titus 2:3, AMPLIFIED).

Of course "older" doesn't only mean those who are chronologically advanced; it can also mean those with more knowledge or wisdom or maturity or life experience.

Elizabeth was just such a godly role model and mentor for Mary. After Mary's encounter with the angel Gabriel, the young woman couldn't wait to go and see the one person she knew who could relate, at least on some level, to her experience. Elizabeth, after all, was expecting her own miracle baby. The moment Mary arrived, Elizabeth knew why she had come. God had shared Mary's secret with her. "Elizabeth was filled with the Holy Spirit. In a loud voice she exclaimed: 'Blessed are you among women, and blessed is the child you will bear! But why am I so favored that the mother of my Lord should come to me? As soon as the sound of your greeting reached my ears, the baby in my womb leaped for joy!'" (Luke 1:42–44).

"I talk in order to understand; I teach in order to learn." —Robert Frost

Then with the authority of a woman who has seen and heard and experienced God's faithfulness for herself, Elizabeth exclaimed to Mary, "Blessed is she who has believed that what the Lord has said to her will be accomplished" (Luke 1:45).

Those words must have brought such comfort and encouragement to a young woman who had felt very much alone. As

Elizabeth shared the truths God had spoken to her own heart, she affirmed Mary—and confirmed the Word of the Lord to her. If Mary had begun to have doubts or fears, Elizabeth dispelled them with her joyous reminder of God's love and faithfulness. And in response, Mary burst forth with a prophetic word of her own—that beautiful psalm of praise we know as "The Magnificat."[1]

We find another example in the book of Ruth. Naomi guided her widowed daughter-in-law not only into the faith, but into a new culture, a new community, and a new husband and family. Their friendship is one of the most heartwarming in all of Scripture.

I can't tell you how thankful I am for the friendship of other women that God has given me. I find there are women I look up to, women whose wisdom and guidance I desperately need, women who are mentors to me—my "spiritual" mothers or grandmothers. They pour into my life the living water they have received. Truthfully, there's very little (if anything) that I can teach them or give them in return. But that doesn't stop them from giving to me and teaching me. I've learned so much from them.

Then there are women who are more like sisters to me. We pour into each other's lives, and we receive from each other. They may have more wisdom or experience in one area; I have it in another. It's what Scripture calls "iron sharpening iron" (see Prov. 27:17). Like David and Jonathan, we help each other "find strength in God" (1 Sam. 23:16).

And then there are women God has called me to minister to, women who, regardless of their chronological age, are in essence my spiritual daughters. I pour into them the living water that God has given me. I mentor them, nurture them, teach them, and train them. Once again, these kinds of relationships are fairly one-sided. In one sense, there isn't much (if anything) that they can teach me or give to me, other than the opportunity to give to them. Though that, in itself, is actually a pretty amazing thing. (If ever I'm tempted to feel even the slightest bit resentful of the sacrifice of my time and energy, I remember how frustrating it is to have something to give and no one to give it to!) We are blessed to be a blessing. "We must help the weak, remembering the words the Lord Jesus himself said: 'It is more blessed to give than to receive'" (Acts 20:35).

Ideally, we all need a balance of all three of these types of friendships or mentoring relationships. If we have too many "filling" relationships, we get spiritually lazy, bloated, overfed. Self-focused. If we have too many "pouring" relationships, we end up empty, exhausted, burned-out.

"Trying to do the Lord's work in your own strength is the most confusing, exhausting, and tedious of all work. But when you are filled with the Holy Spirit, then the ministry of Jesus just flows out of you." —Corrie ten Boom

---

Of course, it does take some effort on our part to seek out and cultivate these types of friendships, to conscientiously and intentionally build these relationships and maintain them. And few of us have only one life-long mentor (or one "BFF"—best friend forever!). Some we have for a season. Or for a particular area of our lives. Eventually we may outgrow some of our mentoring relationships. And that's as it should be. If we've done our job right, our own spiritual daughters will one day grow up and leave the nest. But while we have them, they bring such blessing into our lives.[2]

When we share what we've been given with others, when we teach even practical, ordinary, everyday things, we touch hearts and change lives. We impact not only the person in front of us, but all of the lives they touch—their friends and family, and their friends and family, and their friends and family, in a ripple effect that goes on for all eternity. If we had the slightest inkling, if we could only catch a glimpse of its significance, we would realize in an instant that it is absolutely worth the time, worth the effort, worth the energy, worth the sacrifice.

Christian recording artist Ray Boltz wrote a song about a dream he had in which he was walking the streets of heaven with a dear friend. In the dream, they were approached by a young man who wanted to thank the friend for teaching his Sunday school class when he was eight. It was in Sunday school that he had first prayed and asked Jesus into his heart.

The young man continues, "Thank you for giving to the Lord, I am so glad you gave." One person after another comes forward, as far as the eye could see, each one somehow touched by the kindness, the generosity, the sacrifices of the friend. These things he said and did may have seemed small or inconsequential at the time; they may have gone unnoticed on earth, but in heaven they were being proclaimed.

As the dream (and the song) comes to a close, Ray sings to his friend that although in heaven you're not supposed to cry, "I am almost sure there were tears in your eyes as Jesus took your hand and you stood before the Lord. He said, 'My child look around you, great is your reward.'"[3]

Whenever I hear that song, I think of how I can't wait to get in line, to thank some of the men and women God has used in my own life. I'm so very grateful for the privilege of teaching others what these precious people have taught me.

Bible Study

1. Read the apostle Paul's instructions to young pastor Timothy on how to encourage the women in his congregation in Titus 2:3–5.

a. What special role do "older" women have in the lives of "younger" women (vv. 3-4)?

b. Why do you think that gossip (slander) and a lack of self-control (drunkenness) are particularly inappropriate behaviors for women who are supposed to serve as mentors, confidants, and role models (see Prov. 11:13; Titus 2:7-8, 11-14)?

c. What kinds of things should older and wiser women teach? Practical things? Spiritual things (vv. 4-5)?

d. What happens when new believers and younger members of the body of Christ are not properly discipled, not mentored, *not* taught? On whom does their behavior reflect negatively (v. 5)?

e. Conversely, when all of the women—older and younger—set a good example and teach and train and mentor each other, what happens? To the women themselves? To their local church fellowship? To the community? To the world?

2. What are your biggest struggles right now? Would they fall into the category of self-discipline, organization, relationships, child-rearing, homemaking, career development, or spiritual growth?

Ask the Lord to show you a woman you know who might be able to help you in one or more of these areas. Invite her out for coffee or lunch. With her permission, pick her brain! It could be a one-time thing or the start of an ongoing relationship. If the first woman you approach doesn't have the time or the ability to help you right now, don't be discouraged. Keep looking until you find someone who can!

3. Make a list of your own special skills, spiritual gifts, or personal strengths. What knowledge or expertise do you have that you could share with someone else?

   a. How could you develop your gifts and talents even further?

   b. Who could you share them with? An individual, a small group or class, a community or congregation? Is there a particular age group or specific segment of the population you could serve? Don't forget the members of your own family!

4. Choose one of the following verses (or one mentioned previously in the chapter) to memorize and meditate on this week.

   Deuteronomy 6:6–9   2 Timothy 3:16–17

   Romans 12:6–8   1 Corinthians 9:25–27

   2 Timothy 2:15   James 3:1–2

5. Take a few moments to record any further thoughts or reflections—or a prayer.

Eleven

Words That Ring

"Speak up for those who cannot speak for themselves,
for the rights of all who are destitute." (Prov. 31:8)

Harriet had a pretty hectic life, even by today's standards. Her husband traveled a lot on business, leaving her to run the household and care for their six children. Money was tight; Harriet was always looking for ways to cut corners and bring in extra income. She taught classes at an all-girls academy. She wrote articles for newspapers and magazines. She found she could make even more money writing romance novels, which she did in her "spare" time. Early in the morning before the children woke up or late at night after they'd gone to bed, Harriet picked up her pen and went to work. It was hardly great literature, she knew. But there was a market for these stories, and it did help pay the bills.

Busy as she was, Harriet kept informed about the political and social turmoil going on in the world around her. She couldn't help it. History was being made outside her door. She lived in a "free state" across the river from a "slave state." She frequently saw bounty hunters tracking down runaways in the city streets. Like others in her family, church, and community, Harriet was concerned about the situation; she was deeply troubled by the evil and the injustice she witnessed. But what could one woman do?

"There is in every true woman's heart, a spark of heavenly fire, which lies dormant in the broad daylight of prosperity, but which kindles up and beams and blazes in the dark hour of adversity." —Washington Irving

During the worship service one Sunday morning, Harriet suddenly had a vision. She saw a picture in her mind's eye of an elderly slave being brutally beaten to death. It was heart-rending; she couldn't get the scene out of her mind. Not long afterward, Harriet got a letter from her sister-in-law. It said something along the lines of, "Harriet, I've been thinking. It's obvious you're a gifted writer. (Loved your latest book!) But what if God intended for you to do more with this talent than write romances? What if he gave you this ability so that you could speak out about issues that are so much more important? Issues we both care so much more about . . . like slavery, for instance?"

Harriet's sister-in-law had a way with words. Her gentle encouragement sparked something in Harriet—who also had a way with words. Harriet thought of the vision that had come to her in the church service. She also thought of the pain and heartache she experienced when her youngest child had come down with cholera and died in her arms. She tried to imagine what it would be like to be a slave woman and have her children torn from her arms or to have to witness their suffering, torture, and abuse. Harriet Beecher Stowe started praying for a story that would touch the hearts of men and women all over the world, help them understand the evils of slavery, and cause them to feel compassion. And call them to action.

Uncle Tom's Cabin was published first as a serial story in a newspaper in 1851 then as a novel in 1852. It was soon translated into dozens of languages and became the first book by an American author to sell more than a million copies. In fact, *Uncle Tom's Cabin* would eventually rank as best-selling book of the nineteenth century, second only to the Bible.[1]

And just as the author had hoped, just as she had prayed, quite literally millions of people were moved from apathy and ignorance to passion and action. Historians point to Harriet's novel as one of the most significant cultural events or factors that precipitated the movement to finally end slavery in the United States once and for all. When President Abraham Lincoln was introduced to Harriet, he said, "So you are the little woman who started this great war!"

Throughout history—biblical and otherwise—thousands of women have let their voices ring on behalf of those who could not otherwise be heard. Some of the most revolutionary developments, the most amazing advances in history, science, medicine, education, the arts, civil rights, and cultural and family values have been made by women on a mission. Women who saw evil or injustice or inequality and refused to keep quiet about it. Women who would not let conventional wisdom—the status quo—go unchallenged.

Thousands, if not millions, more have been stirred, inspired, motivated, and galvanized into action by these women's impassioned pleas. For every famous figure and every household name, there are countless other unsung heroes. Women whose names you and I will never know, but who have, nonetheless, worked tirelessly to raise awareness in their own neighborhoods, workplaces, and communities.

Then of course, there are all the wives who said something to their husbands or the mothers who remarked to their sons or daughters some little thing that lit a fire in their souls. Women like Harriet's sister-in-law.

"Fighting is essentially a masculine idea; a woman's weapon is her tongue." —Hermione Gingold

---

There are so many problems in the world today, so many challenges we face. Hunger. Disease. Homelessness. Illiteracy. Domestic violence. Child Abuse. Prostitution and sex trafficking. Pornography. Gambling. Substance abuse and addiction. Eating disorders. Suicide. Racism and discrimination. The rights of the unborn. The needs of the elderly and the disabled. The list goes on and on. The causes that speak to us may vary greatly, as do the ways we speak for them. But unquestionably, we are all called in one way or another to speak up, to speak out. It couldn't be more biblical.

Scripture says, "Rescue those being led away to death; hold back those staggering toward slaughter. If you say, 'But we knew nothing about this,' does not he who weighs the heart perceive it? Does not he who guards your life know it? Will he not repay each person according to what he has done?" (Prov. 24:11–12).

God says ignorance is not an excuse. Apathy is unacceptable. We *are* our brothers' and sisters' keepers. We cannot look the other way. We are called to be a voice for the voiceless, a help to the helpless. We are to stand up to evil wherever we find it, rescue those held captive or oppressed, and fight to our last breath to defend the cause of the innocent. We cannot excuse ourselves by saying we didn't see or we didn't know. God sees.

God knows. And he who weighs our hearts will one day call us to account.

The book of Judges tells us the story of one woman who chose not to sit on the sidelines—or "under a palm tree"—when a national crisis called for action: "Deborah, a prophetess, the wife of Lappidoth, was leading Israel at that time. She held court under the Palm of Deborah between Ramah and Bethel in the hill country of Ephraim, and the Israelites came to her to have their disputes decided" (Judg. 4:4–5).

One day, God gave Deborah a message for Barak, commander of the armies of Israel. At last, the Lord was ready to destroy the heathen nation that had oppressed his people for more than twenty years. God wanted Barak to ride out against Sisera, commander of the Canaanites, and engage him in battle at Mount Tabor. But Barak wasn't very brave—or else he was very superstitious. In awe of Deborah's spiritual discernment, the special connection she seemed to have with God, Barak insisted that he would not set one foot in the direction of Mount Tabor unless Deborah promised to go with him.

Now whoever heard of a general refusing to send his troops into battle unless a woman (a wife and a mother, no less) led the way? It was ludicrous, ridiculous, even to Deborah herself. Yet God's Word must be obeyed, his purposes accomplished, and his will be done. So Deborah acquiesced to Barak's request.

"'Very well,' Deborah said, 'I will go with you. But because of the way you are going about this, the honor will not be yours, for the Lord will hand Sisera over to a woman . . .'" (Judg. 4:9).

As the battle was about to begin, it seems Barak was still wavering in his resolve, still needing encouragement and reassurance. So Deborah, perhaps a little impatiently, said to him: "Go! This is the day the Lord has given Sisera into your hands. Has not the Lord gone ahead of you? . . ." (Judg. 4:14).

God was true to His Word; he gave his people the victory. But it was not Barak or any of his soldiers who killed the commander of the enemy army. That honor belonged to another "housewife"—Jael, who sweetly invited Sisera to avoid capture by hiding in her tent and then drove a peg through his head.

Then there's the story of Esther, the orphaned Jewish girl who won the most famous beauty pageant of all time. Through a miraculous series of events, she was chosen to be the bride of King Xerxes—ruler of the Babylonian Empire. Esther's cousin Mordecai learned of a sinister plot to annihilate the entire Jewish race. Mordecai called on Esther to approach the king on behalf of her people, to beseech him for mercy and protection.

> "A woman is like a tea bag—you never know how strong she is until she gets in hot water." —Eleanor Roosevelt

At first, the young queen was flabbergasted at the thought, completely overwhelmed by the magnitude of the request, doubtful of the outcome of such an enterprise. She would quite literally be taking her life into her own hands. But Esther's cousin admonished her to recognize the responsibility that comes with privilege. To whom much is given, much will be required (see Luke 12:48). Neither the role of innocent victim nor helpless bystander was an option for the queen. "Do not think that because you are in the king's house you alone of all the Jews will escape" (Est. 4:13).

Esther had not chosen to go into battle, but the battle had come to her. She needed to understand that God had not given her the privileges of royalty to make her happy or keep her comfortable or entertained. He had allowed Esther to become queen and placed her in the palace for this very moment, this very crisis. God had a plan to deliver his people, and he wanted to use Esther to accomplish it. Mordecai told Esther that if she refused, he was sure God would find another way—but her disobedience would no doubt cost her dearly. "For if you keep silent at this time, relief and deliverance for the Jews will arise from another place, but you and your father's house will perish. And who knows whether you have not come to the kingdom for such a time as this?" (Est. 4:14).

One of the things that strikes me about these two women— Deborah and Esther—is the contrast between them. Deborah was obviously a very articulate, educated woman. She had to be, having been chosen by the people themselves to rule over all Israel and to administer justice, to teach God's law and explain to his people how to apply it to their circumstances.

Esther, on the other hand, went to beauty school. It's unlikely she knew how to read or write; matters of state were certainly beyond her scope of expertise.

When the courage of men failed, Deborah rose to the occasion and rode into battle without hesitation. She was the original "warrior princess"; she relished the opportunity to devastate the enemies of God. (Read her uproariously joyful and triumphant victory chant in Judges 5!)

Esther was shaking in her shoes just thinking about approaching her admittedly psychotic husband. It was, after all, *against the law* for her to appear before him without an invitation or prior permission. She was terrified, absolutely worried sick about what she was going to say. But she did it.

"When I see the elaborate study and ingenuity displayed by women in the pursuit of trifles, I feel no doubt of their capacity for the most Herculean undertakings." —Julia Ward Howe

By all outward appearances, these women were unlikely heroes. On the surface they seemed powerless, but in reality, they were powerful. God's grace was sufficient for them; his power was made perfect in their weakness (2 Cor. 12:9). And that same grace is available to us today. It's the grace by which we stand (Rom. 5:1–5).

Some of us taken dozens of little stands every day. (I'm thinking, for instance, of the women I know who gently but firmly request that their coworkers not use the name of "the Person most precious" to them as a swear word.) We can't possibly know just how significant these "little" stands are, what eternal impact they might have. Others of us find ourselves faced, perhaps just once in our lives, with a real "do or die" moment—a time when we must choose to speak now or forever hold our peace. Still others are permanently stationed on the front lines of a major battlefield, called to give everything we are and everything we hold dear—even our very lives—for a cause greater than ourselves.

"Although the world is full of suffering, it is also full of the overcoming of it." —Helen Keller

Whatever our task, whatever our role, whatever our responsibility before God, there are at least six things we all need.

(1)We need a vision, an understanding of our own calling. We need a passion for the people on whose behalf God has chosen us to speak, those he has particularly chosen *us* to protect and defend, those for whom we must speak up and speak out. They may be in our schools, our neighborhoods, or our churches. They may be hundreds, even thousands of miles away, on a different continent, or in a different country or culture. Only God himself can reveal to each one of us individually what his vision, his calling, is for us. And only he can rouse us from the apathy, complacency, and indifference that so often plagues us.

As former United States Senate Chaplain Peter Marshall (husband of author Catherine Marshall) once observed, "A different world cannot be built by indifferent people."

(2) We need guidance to know what—if anything—we can do to better inform ourselves or better prepare ourselves for the task ahead. Often we find that God himself has been preparing us all along. Our background, our personality, our life experiences, our skills and talents, and our special interests all come together to make us the perfect person for the job! Then again, God sometimes stretches us by putting us in a position we feel completely unqualified for. It means we have to lean hard on him. We must do everything in our power to figure out what things we need to learn, what skills we need to acquire, which gifts we need to develop to better serve our calling—and our Creator.

(3) We need a willingness to make the sacrifices that are necessary to answer God's call—and clear direction as to what those sacrifices are. How can we make more of our time and energy and resources available to God? Are we willing to risk our reputation, our career, our social standing? Could we give up our comfort and security? If called upon to lay down our lives for this cause, would we? Jesus said, "Blessed are you when men hate you, when they exclude you and insult you and reject your name as evil, because of the Son of Man. Rejoice in that day and leap for joy, because great is your reward in heaven . . ." (Luke 6:22–23). And again, "If anyone would come after me, he must deny himself and take up his cross daily and follow me. For whoever wants to save his life will lose it, but whoever loses his life for me will save it. What good is it for a man to gain the whole world, and yet lose or forfeit his very self?" (Luke 9:23–25). To paraphrase martyred missionary Jim Elliot, "She is no fool who gives what she cannot keep to gain that which she cannot lose."

(4) We need wisdom to know what to say and when to say it. In other words, we need a sensitivity to the leading of the Holy Spirit. Remember that Esther didn't blurt out her request when

she first approached her husband in the throne room—or at the first banquet she invited him to (Est. 5:1–8). Before Abigail pleaded her case to David, she paved the way with a generous and thoughtful gift (1 Sam. 25:18–19). There's most certainly a time to be direct and straightforward, a time to be honest, blunt, and even confrontational. There's also a time for civility, gentility, and skillful diplomacy. Some messages work best as sermons, others as stories (see 2 Sam. 12:1–13).

(5) We need wisdom to know where and how God wants us to speak. Should it be spontaneous—by "divine appointment"— or by invitation? Person-to-person contact, one-on-one? Or do we take the platform at our churches or civic groups, in town halls or PTA meetings? Do we write letters to the editor? Lobby congress? Run for office? Should we start a blog or a Web site or an e-zine? Create a foundation or a nonprofit organization? Or do we write a song, poem, book, Bible study, or novel with a message that (like Harriet's) has the potential to touch hearts and lives around the world?

(6) We need courage, a holy boldness. In a song called "Run to the Battle," Christian recording artist Steve Camp says, "Some people want to live within the sound of chapel bells, but I want to run a mission a yard from the gates of hell." Now that's holy boldness. I have to admit I more often identify with J. R. R. Tolkien's hobbit hero, Frodo, in The Lord of the Rings. Frodo sees that the lines have been drawn for the ultimate battle of good and evil. And the good are terribly outnumbered. The growing darkness—the corruption of what was once good and true—is oppressive. His quest to destroy the evil ring of power seems hopeless.

"I wish the ring had never come to me," Frodo exclaims. "I wish none of this had ever happened." His friend Gandalf replies, "So do all who live to see such times, but that is not for them to decide. All we have to decide is what to do with the time that is given to us."

Reading through the letters to the early church in the New Testament, we can tell that many of those first disciples felt the same discouragement as Frodo. Hard-pressed on every side, persecuted, suffering—they struggled to hold on to hope in the face of overwhelming evil. But the apostles reminded them of the ultimate victory that was theirs in Christ and challenged them in the meantime to stand fast, to fight the good fight, and to make "the most of every opportunity, because the days are evil" (Eph. 5:16).

"Be strong in the Lord and in his mighty power. Put on the full armor of God so that you can take your stand against the devil's schemes" (Eph. 6:10–11). Win as many battles as you can! "Live holy and godly lives as you look forward to the day of God and speed its coming" (2 Pet. 3:11–12)!

At times we may feel overwhelmed by the challenges we face. The task we've been given seems too hard, the cost too high. But we must remember that we've been blessed with the incredible privilege of being servants of the Most High. And God has put us where we are for a reason. When we look to him, we will find all the wisdom and strength we need to accomplish his purposes. For we, too, are called—for such a time as this.

Bible Study

1. With the help of her cousin Mordecai, Esther came to realize that God himself had made her queen—that he had put her in the position to help her people in their greatest time of need, "for such a time as this." Read her response to this revelation in Esther 4:15–16.

   a. Esther knew that she could not win this battle alone; she needed help. Who did she ask to stand with her (v. 16a)?

b. What did she ask them to do? Who were they turning to (v. 16a)?

c. What did Esther herself do, in preparation for the task ahead of her (v. 16b)?

d. What did Esther say to indicate her total commitment, her willingness to make the ultimate sacrifice in obedience to the Lord (v. 16c)?

e. Where did Esther's courage and strength come from? Where do you think she got the unusual strategy, the unorthodox "battle plan," described in Esther 5:1–8?

f. How important was her timing—the decision to reveal her request to the king when she did? What did God do in the intervening time to make the king favorably disposed to grant her request (see the events that transpired in Est. 6:1–11)?

g. What was the end result (7:9–10; 8:11)?

If you can answer the following questions immediately, then do so. Otherwise, spend some time in prayer asking God over the next few moments or days (weeks or months, if necessary) to reveal the answers to you.

2. What vision or calling or passion has God given you? What causes capture your interest? What concerns motivate you to act? What needs move you to tears?

3. What's keeping you from walking in this calling or giving yourself more fully to the cause? What do you most need?

- [ ] Further clarity about the true nature of the task at hand or the role God wants you to play.

- [ ] Guidance as to what steps to take to better inform yourself or prepare yourself for the task.

- [ ] Willingness to make the sacrifices necessary.

- [ ] Direction as to how to make more of your time, energy, and resources available for God's use.

- [ ] Wisdom to know what to say, when to say it, and how to say it.

- [ ] Holy boldness; the courage to step out in faith and speak up.

- [ ] Open doors and opportunities to speak out.

James 1:5 says, "If you need wisdom, ask our generous God, and he will give it to you . . ." (NLT). Philippians 4:19 reminds us, "God will meet all your needs according to his glorious riches in Christ Jesus." Ask God to give you whatever it is that you need today.

4. Choose one of the following verses (or one mentioned previously in the chapter) to memorize and meditate on this week.

Proverbs 31:8–9a	Matthew 10:32
Isaiah 58:1–11	1 Peter 3:14–16
Matthew 10:18–20	1 John 3:16

5. Take a few moments to record any further thoughts or reflections.

Twelve

Words Aren't Everything

"If the pen is mightier than the sword, then how can actions speak louder than words?"

Women have a way with words: words that wound, words that heal, words that reveal; words that live, words that die, words that sing, words that cry; words that reach, words that teach, words that ring. But words aren't everything, especially when they're empty or insincere. Or when they aren't followed by action. James, who had so much to say about the power of the tongue, pointed out this paradox himself: "Suppose a brother or sister is without clothes and daily food. If one of you says to him, 'Go, I wish you well; keep warm and well fed,' but does nothing about his physical needs, what good is it?" (James 2:15–16). Those words become meaningless.

John concurs, "Let's not merely say that we love each other; let us show the truth by our actions" (1 John 3:18, NLT). The reality is that we must both speak *and* act in accordance with the truth we have received from God (James 2:12). Otherwise,

157

James says, we deceive ourselves and our religion is worthless (James 1:22–27).

Jesus once told a story about a man who had two sons. The man went to the first one and said, "Son, go and work today in the vineyard." The first son refused. "'I will not,' he answered, but later he changed his mind and went. Then the father went to the other son and said the same thing. He answered, 'I will, sir,' but he did not go." Jesus asked the crowd gathered around him, "Which of the two did what his father wanted?" "The first," they answered (Matt. 21:28–31).

> "We have too many high sounding words, and too few actions that correspond with them." —Abigail Adams

Jesus used this story to point out to the Pharisees—the pompous, pious religious leaders of the day—that God wants more from us than lip service. We may know all the right words to say. And we may say them at the right time and in the right way. But do we really mean them?

For example, do we really love our heavenly Father and want to do his will? Sometimes our lips say yes, but our lives say no. We are a walking contradiction, and our words—no matter how carefully chosen, no matter how well-intended—will be meaningless to our hearers, because they see the duplicity, the hypocrisy. If we want our words to have power and meaning and significance, if we want them to make a positive impact on the world around us, then we have to get our lives in line with those words. We have got to get real. Now.

But there's another moral to the story we can't afford to miss. Remember that first son? The one who, in essence, threw a tantrum and refused to do what his father asked him to? It turns out that when all was said and done he was the hero of the story.

He was the obedient son! He had the courage to admit that he was wrong, that his attitude—his heart—wasn't right. And he didn't just feel bad about it. He didn't slink off into a corner to hide. He didn't wallow in his guilt. He got up and went out to the vineyard and started working. In the end, he did the job his father asked him to do.

What a wonderful reminder that it's not too late for any of us to be the loving, obedient children that, deep down, we long to be. Especially when it comes to the way we use our words—the way we exercise this precious gift of power and influence that we have been given. We've made some mistakes in the past, for sure. Maybe a lot of mistakes. And we will surely make more in the future. But we can't let that keep us from doing our very best today, making the most of the opportunities we've been given today.

"Sometimes we don't need another chance to express how we feel or to ask someone to understand our situation. Sometimes we just need a firm kick in the pants. An unsmiling expectation that if we mean all these wonderful things we talk about and sing about, then let's see something to prove it." —Dietrich Bonhoeffer

The apostle Paul admitted that he wasn't perfect, by any means; he didn't claim to have "arrived." He wrestled with the sin in his life on a daily basis, just as we do. Still, he wasn't about to allow his present faults and past failures to keep him from making any progress in his spiritual journey— in the "race" of faith: "One thing I do: Forgetting what is behind and straining toward what is ahead, I press on toward the goal to win the prize for which God has called me heavenward in Christ Jesus" (Phil. 3:13–14).

Each and every day there are new opportunities to speak the kinds of words that honor God. Words that uplift and encourage and inspire others. Words that challenge and motivate, guide and teach. Words that have the power to touch the hearts and lives of those around us for all eternity. Each and every day we have new opportunities to put our words into action and live them out in front of others. We've spent a lot of time together reflecting on what God says about what we say, what his Word teaches us about ours. It's time to put those truths into practice: "Do not merely listen to the Word. . . . Do what it says" (James 1:22).

> "When I had forgotten God, yet I then found He had not forgotten me. Even then He did by His Spirit apply the merits of the great atonement to my soul, by telling me that Christ died for me." —Susanna Wesley

Jesus told another story, another parable about a man who was called away on business and left his servants behind to manage his resources and take care of his property (Matt. 25:14–30). When the man gave them their assignments, he took into account their individual temperament and personality, their level of experience, wisdom, and maturity, and their natural ability.

"To one he gave five talents . . . to another two talents, and to another one talent . . ." (Matt. 25:15). In those days, a talent was a particular sum of money. (Today, we call a gift that someone has been given to use for his own benefit and the benefit of others a "talent" because of this biblical story.)

The man who had received the five talents immediately invested the money in a sound business venture and quickly doubled it. Likewise, the one with the two talents found a way to multiply the two into four. But for some reason, the man who had received the one talent went off, dug a hole in the ground, and hid his master's money.

The owner was gone for a very long time. When he returned, he was eager to hear how his servants had looked after his property and what they had done with the talents—the resources— he had left in their care.

"The man who had received the five talents brought the other five. 'Master,' he said, 'you entrusted me with five talents. See, I have gained five more.'"

His master was very pleased. "Well done, good and faithful servant! You have been faithful with a few things; I will put you in charge of many things. Come and share your master's happiness!"

Then the man with the two talents came forward. "'Master,' he said, 'you entrusted me with two talents; see, I have gained two more.'"

> "How wonderful it is that nobody need
> wait a single moment before starting
> to improve the world." —Anne Frank

Again, his master was very pleased. "Well done, good and faithful servant! You have been faithful with a few things; I will put you in charge of many things. Come and share your master's happiness!" Note that there was no complaint that the two-talent profit was less than the five-talent profit. Each man had simply done his best with what he had been given; the master expected no more and no less.

Then the man who had received the one talent came forward—probably rather sheepishly. When he saw what the other servants had done with their talents, he likely realized what he should have done. His lack of initiative, his laziness, his irresponsibility was about to be exposed. Instead of admitting his mistake, instead of apologizing and asking for a second chance, he made excuses. He tried to shift the blame—onto his master, of all people! He called the master a hard and unforgiving taskmaster and said he was afraid of all the trouble he would get into if he failed. That's why the man did nothing with the talent. That's why he hid it and buried it in the ground.

"Do all the good you can, by all the means you can, in all the ways you can, in all the places you can, at all the times you can, to all the people you can, as long as ever you can." —John Wesley

His master saw right through the third man's excuses. And he didn't appreciate the insult implied in the accusation. The very least this servant could have done was put the money in the bank. Then it would have earned some interest. The talent was taken away from the unfaithful servant immediately and given to one of the others. As for the servant himself, he was thrown off the property—sent away in shame and disgrace.

There are many different gifts, different talents that God has given each one of us. Here I want to focus on the one that, as women, we share: a way with words. Some of us are more articulate than others; some have a greater sphere of influence or a louder voice. But whether the measure of our talent is great or small, whether our opportunities to use this talent are many or (comparatively) few, what God asks is that we do our best.

That we nurture and develop and exercise this talent to the best of our ability. That we don't sit on it or silence it, but that we put it to use. For his glory and the greater good.

To use the vineyard analogy, our job is to plant the seeds where and when and how he tells us to. We are to water them, to nurture them, and to help them grow. God is the one who will produce the harvest, the fruit.

One day, we may just find a line of people waiting to speak to us in heaven, waiting to share how something we said or something we did made a difference in their lives. Some we will know and remember right away. Others will be a complete surprise. But best of all, we'll get to hear the words that Jesus will say to *us*: "Well done, good and faithful servant. Well done, precious daughter. Welcome to the celebration! Wait till you see what I have in store for you here!"

Bible Study

1. Read John 14–15. In John 14:15, Jesus said, "If you love me, you will obey what I command."

   a. What does he promise those who love and obey him? (14:21, 23)?

   b. How does he say we will be able to understand and remember his commands (14:26)?

   c. What name does Jesus give himself in John 15:1?

   d. What does he call us (15:5)?

   e. What has he chosen us and called us to do (15:16)?

   f. What does this look like (see Gal. 5:22–23)?

   g. How can we do what he asks? How can we produce what he wants to see (John 15:4–5)?

h. What do we need to watch out for (Song 2:15)?

i. What do these "pests" look like in your own life? What threatens your connection to the True Vine or keeps you from being as fruitful as he intends for you to be?

2. If you had to choose one thing that God has shown you through this study, one thing you've learned about the power of your words, or one area in which you've been particularly convicted or challenged or motivated or inspired, what would it be?

3. How can you turn these words into action? How can you put this truth into practice and apply what you've learned to your life today?

4. Choose one of the following verses (or one mentioned previously in the chapter) to memorize and meditate on this week.

Isaiah 1:18	1 John 1:6–7
Lamentations 3:21–23	1 John 1:8–9
Lamentations 3:40	1 John 5:3–4
Mark 12:30	1 John 5:14–15
James 1:2–4	

5. Write a prayer of commitment, asking God to keep the truth that he has shown you on your mind and in your heart continually, from now on.

Recommended Resources

Understanding Our God-Given Influence and Making the Most of It

100 Christian Women Who Changed the 20ᵗʰ Century by Helen Kooiman Hosier (Revell, 2000).

Becoming a Woman of Influence: Making a Lasting Impact on Others by Carol Kent (NavPress, 2006).

Becoming God's True Woman, edited by Nancy Leigh DeMoss (Crossway, 2008).

The Language of Love and Respect: Cracking the Communication Code with Your Mate by Emerson Eggerichs (Thomas Nelson, 2009).

Faces of Faith, edited by Jon Hanna (Bridge-Logos, 2006).

The Friendships of Women: The Beauty and Power of God's Plan for Us, revised and updated by Dee Brestin (David C. Cook, 2008).

Mothers of Influence: The Inspiring Stories of Women Who Made a Difference in Their Children and Their World, compiled by Heartland Editorial Management (Honor Books, 2005).

Now You're Speaking My Language: Honest Communication and Deeper Intimacy for a Stronger Marriage by Gary Chapman (B & H Publishing, 2007).

The Power of a Positive Mom, revised edition by Karol Ladd (Howard, 2007).

The Power of a Positive Wife by Karol Ladd (Howard, 2003).

The Power of a Positive Woman by Karol Ladd (Howard, 2002).
Simple Little Words: What You Say Can Change a Life by Michelle Cox and John Perrodin (Honor Books, 2008).
What Happens When Women Say Yes to God by Lysa Terkeurst (Harvest House, 2007).
You Matter More Than You Think: What a Woman Needs to Know about the Difference She Makes by Leslie Parrott (Zondervan, 2006).

Recovering from Words That Have Wounded Us

Choosing Forgiveness: Your Journey to Freedom by Nancy Leigh DeMoss (Moody, 2006).
The Emotionally Destructive Relationship: Seeing It, Stopping It, Surviving It by Leslie Vernick (Harvest House, 2007).
God Meant It for Good, third edition, by R. T. Kendall (Morningstar, 2003).
Wounded by Words: Healing the Invisible Scars of Emotional Abuse by Susan Titus Osborn, Karen L. Kosman, and Jeenie Gordon (New Hope, 2008).
Your Scars Are Beautiful to God: Finding Peace and Purpose in the Hurts of Your Past by Sharon Jaynes (Harvest House, 2006).

Growing in Our Understanding of and Appreciation for the Word of God

A Family Guide to the Bible by Christin Ditchfield (Crossway, 2009).
Grasping God's Word: A Hands-On Approach to Reading, Interpreting, and Applying the Bible by J. Scott Duvall and J. Daniel Hays (Zondervan, 2005).
How to Study Your Bible by Kay Arthur (Harvest House, 1994).
A Place of Quiet Rest: Finding Intimacy with God through a Daily Devotional Life by Nancy Leigh DeMoss (Moody, 2000).
Sacred Pathways: Discover Your Soul's Path to God by Gary Thomas (Zondervan, 2000).

Sharing Our Hearts with God in Praise and Worship and Prayer

Live a Praying Life: Open Your Life to God's Power and Provision by Jennifer Kennedy Dean (New Hope, 2004).

The Power of a Praying Parent by Stormie Omartian (Harvest House, 2005).

The Power of a Praying Wife by Stormie Omartian (Harvest House, 1997).

The Power of a Praying Woman by Stormie Omartian (Harvest House, 2002).

A Woman of Worship by Dee Brestin (David C. Cook, 2005).

When Women Worship: Creating an Atmosphere of Intimacy with God by Amie Dockery and Mary Alessi (Regal, 2007).

Developing Our Teaching/Training/Leadership Ability

Building an Effective Women's Ministry by Sharon Jaynes (Harvest House, 2005).

Communication Plus: How to Speak So People Will Listen by Marita Littauer and Florence Littauer (Regal, 2006).

Leading Women to the Heart of God by Lysa Terkeurst (Moody, 2002).

Leading Women Who Wound: Strategies for an Effective Ministry by Sue Edwards and Kelley Matthews (Moody, 2009).

Speak up with Confidence: A Step by Step Guide for Speakers and Leaders, revised and updated by Carol Kent (NavPress, 2007).

Spiritual Mothering: The Titus 2 Model for Women Mentoring Women by Susan Hunt (Crossway, 1992).

Woman to Woman: Preparing Yourself to Mentor by Edna Ellison and Tricia Scribner (New Hope, 2005).

Women Helping Women: A Biblical Guide to Major Issues Women Face by Elyse Fitzpatrick and Carol Cornish (Harvest House, 1997).

Acknowledgments

In writing a book like this, I can't help but be mindful of the many women God has used to speak so powerfully into my own heart and life. There are those who came into my life for a moment—a brief, but very significant moment—"for such a time as this." There are some who were sent for a season. And there are some who are now and always will be my "forever" friends. There are those I've known personally and intimately, and those I've never met—some who may even have died years before I was born, and yet whose testimonies and wise words have challenged me and encouraged me and inspired me all the days of my life. I wish I could list them all here (and part of me desperately wants to try), but I know in my heart it just isn't possible. There are too many! And I would be sure to accidentally leave some out. I can only thank God whenever I think of these precious women, pray that he will bless them abundantly beyond all they can ask or even think, and try to be a living tribute—a true reflection of all that they taught me, as well as the One they pointed me to.

While I was working on this book, I faced some of the greatest physical challenges of my life—surgery after surgery after surgery, followed by months and months and *months* of bed rest and physical therapy—all of which took a toll on me mentally, emotionally, and spiritually. I want to express my gratitude to everyone at Crossway (especially Jill Carter) for their faithful prayers, constant encouragement, and unwavering support, not to mention their extraordinary patience when I missed deadline after deadline. Thank you for not giving up on me or this book.

Thank you to those precious friends who lifted me up and carried me to Jesus, day after day (Mark 2:1–4). And a very special thank-you to those who offered to read the early chapters as they were written (partly to motivate me to get back to work!) and then insisted that I couldn't give up—I had to finish—because they wanted to read the rest. Your words have meant more to me than you will ever know.

About the Author

Christin Ditchfield is an accomplished educator, author, conference speaker, and host of the syndicated radio program, Take It To Heart!® heard daily on hundreds of stations across the United States and around the world. Using real life stories, rich word pictures, biblical illustrations, and touches of humor, Christin calls believers to enthusiastically seek after God, giving them practical tools to help deepen their personal relationship with Christ.

Christin has written dozens of best-selling gospel tracts and hundreds of columns, essays, and articles for numerous national and international magazines, such as *Focus on the Family*, *Today's Christian*, *Sports Spectrum*, and *Power for Living*. She is the author of more than fifty books, including *A Family Guide to Narnia*, *A Family Guide to the Bible*, *Take It To Heart*, and *The Three Wise Women: A Christmas Reflection*. A frequent guest on radio and television programs such as "Open Line," "Midday Connection," "Prime Time America," "Truth Talk Live," "HomeWord" with Jim Burns, and Dr. D. James Kennedy's "Truths That Transform," Christin holds a masters degree in biblical theology from Southwestern Assemblies of God University in Waxahachie, TX.

For more information, please visit her Web site: www.TakeIt ToHeartRadio.com.

Notes

Chapter 1: Women Have a Way with Words

1. Letter from Walter Reed to Emilie B. Lawrence, August 19, 1875 [01644001]. From the Philip S. Hench Walter Reed Yellow Fever Collection at the University of Virginia, http://etext.virginia.edu/healthsci/reed/.

2. James Dobson, *Love for a Lifetime: Building a Marriage That Will Go the Distance* (Sisters, OR: Multnomah, 1993), 57.

Chapter 2: Words That Wound

1. Corrie ten Boom, *I'm Still Learning to Forgive* (Wheaton, IL: Good News, 1995). Full text available at Good News and Crossway, http://www.crossway.org/product/663575723080/.

Chapter 4: Words That Reveal

1. Anne Bradstreet (1612–1672), "Upon the Burning of Our House." Spelling modernized for clarity.

2. If some of the phrases in the poem sound familiar, they should. Anne's heart drew its comfort and guidance from the words of Scripture. She referred to at least seven different passages in this poem, including Job 1:21, Ecclesiastes 1:2, 2 Chronicles 32:8, Jeremiah 17:5–7, 2 Corinthians 5:1, Hebrews 11:10, and Luke 12:22–34.

3. Hannah Hurnard, *Mountains of Spices* (Wheaton, IL: Tyndale, 1977), 142–43.

Chapter 6: Words That Die

1. From The Westminster Confession of Faith and Larger Catechism (1646): Question 145: "What are the sins forbidden in the ninth commandment?" Answer: "The sins forbidden in the ninth commandment are, all prejudicing the truth, and the good name of our neighbors, as well as our own, especially in public judicature; giving false evidence, suborning false witnesses, wittingly appearing and pleading for an evil cause, outfacing and overbearing the truth; passing unjust sentence, calling evil good, and good evil; rewarding the wicked according to the work of the righteous, and the righteous according to the work of the wicked; forgery, concealing the truth, undue silence in a just cause, and holding our peace when iniquity calls for either a reproof from ourselves, or complaint to others; speaking the truth unseasonably, or maliciously to a wrong end, or perverting it to a wrong meaning, or in doubtful and equivocal expressions, to the prejudice of truth or justice; speaking untruth, lying, slandering, backbiting, detracting, tale bearing, whispering, scoffing, reviling, rash, harsh, and partial censuring; misconstructing intentions, words, and actions; flattering, vainglorious boasting, thinking or speaking too highly or too meanly of ourselves or others; denying the gifts and graces of God; aggravating smaller faults; hiding, excusing, or extenuating of sins, when called to a free confession; unnecessary discovering of infirmities; raising false rumors, receiving and countenancing evil reports, and stopping our ears against just defense; evil suspicion; envying or grieving at the deserved credit of any, endeavoring or desiring to impair it, rejoicing in their disgrace and infamy; scornful contempt, fond admiration; breach of lawful promises; neglecting such things as are of good report, and practicing, or not avoiding ourselves, or not hindering what we can in others, such things as procure an ill name."

2. Sir Walter Scott, *Marmion*, Canto VI, Stanza XVII.

Chapter 7: Words That Sing

1. Elizabeth Barrett Browning, *Aurora Leigh* (New York: C. S. Francis & Co., 1857), 275.

2. Horatio G. Spafford, "It Is Well with My Soul, 1873.

3. Holocaust victim Betsie ten Boom, quoted in *Amazing Love*, by Corrie ten Boom (Grand Rapids, MI: Revell, 1999), 9–10.

Chapter 8: Word That Cry

1. C. S. Lewis, *The Magician's Nephew* (New York: HarperCollins, 1955), 178.

2. Elizabeth Barrett Browning, *Aurora Leigh* (New York: C. S. Francis & Co., 1857), 70.

3. Suzanne Gaither Jennings and Bonnie Keen, "When God Says No," © 2003, Julie Rose Music, Inc. (ASCAP) Townsend and Warbucks Music (ASCAP), administered by Gaither Copyright Management, Inc.

Chapter 9: Words That Reach

1. Some of these key Scriptures include those in the "Roman Road" (Rom. 3:23; 6:23; 5:8; 10:9–10, 13), and verses such as Hebrews 9:27; Ephesians 2:8–9; John 3:16; Acts 4:12; and Acts 16:30–31.

Chapter 10: Words That Teach

1. I've written more on the special relationship shared by Mary and Elizabeth in *The Three Wise Women: A Christmas Reflection*, published by Crossway, 2005.

2. In her book *The Mentor Quest* (Ann Arbor, MI: Vine Books, 2002), author and Bible teacher Betty Southard reminds us that not everyone is able to find the right person to mentor them, someone willing and able to invest her time and energy. Some of us are isolated (geographically or otherwise) and have limited contact with the kind of women who can be our role models and mentors on a daily basis. But we can be mentored by the women whose books we read, whose teaching we listen to, whose lives we study, and whose examples we follow—women of the Bible, women of historical significance, and/or contemporary Christian teachers and leaders. I have certainly found this to be true in my own life.

3. Ray Boltz, "Thank You," © 1988, Gaither Music / ASCAP.

Chapter 11: Words That Ring

1. As noted in the article "Uncle Tom's Cabin," by Joy Jordan-Lake, featured in *A Faith and Culture Devotional: Daily Readings on Art, Science, and Life* by Lael Arrington and Kelly Monroe Kullberg (Grand Rapids, MI: Zondervan, 2008), 267–68.